HEADS UP!

HEADS UP!

SPORTS DEVOTIONS FOR ALL-STAR KIDS

DAVE BRANON

ZONDERVAN.com/
AUTHORTRACKER
follow your favorite authors

ZONDERKIDZ

Heads Up!

Copyright © 2012 by Dave Branon

This title is also available as a Zondervan ebook.
Visit www.zondervan.com/ebooks.

Requests for information should be addressed to:
Zonderkidz, 5300 Patterson Ave SE, Grand Rapids, Michigan 49530

Library of Congress Cataloging-in-Publication Data

Branon, Dave.
      Heads up! : sports devotions for all-star kids / Dave Branon. — [Updated ed.]
        p. cm.
     ISBN 978-0-310-72544-2 (softcover)
     1. Children—Prayers and devotions—Juvenile literature. 2. Sports—Religious
aspects—Christianity—Juvenile literature. I. Title.
    BV4870.B68 2012
    242'.62—dc23

                                                      2011036688

Editor: Kim Childress
Cover design: Kris Nelson
Interior design: Ben Fetterly

Printed in the United States of America

---

13 14 15 16 17 18 19 /QVR/ 20 19 18 17 16 15 14 13 12 11 10 9 8 7 6 5 4 3 2 1

Introduction

I needed somebody to give me a "Heads Up!" a couple of times during my days as an athlete—but it didn't happen.

One time I took a baseball right in the nose because the ball came my way without anyone bothering to yell, "Heads up!" I was just eleven years old or so at the time, but I still remember how much it hurts to have a baseball rearrange your face.

Another time, I was playing college basketball when a player on the other team ran into me and split my chin open with his head. Again, I wish one of my buddies would have warned me with a "Heads up!" before we collided.

It's good to get a "heads up" call. Let's say you're sitting in the box seats at a baseball game, and you turn your head to holler at the hot dog guy to bring you a couple of red hots. Suddenly, some Albert Pujols wannabe nails a high fastball and pulls it down the third baseline—right at your bean. As the ball locks in on your noggin', someone a few seats away screams, "Heads up!"

You know the drill. You duck and cover your head with your hands to protect your skull. The ball glances off your arm and bounces harmlessly to a guy about five rows away, who keeps it. At least he could offer you the ball, but hey, nobody's perfect.

In that kind of "heads up" situation, you are grateful for those two words.

That's what I want this spiritual "heads up!" to do for you.

Get Your Attention

Sometimes our attention gets turned away from God a little bit, and we need someone to wake us up before we get hammered with some problem we didn't see coming. That's one thing *Heads Up!* can do for you—get you thinking about God in the middle of all the other stuff going on in your life.

There's another way to look at the term "heads up!" Sometimes we can get a little down about life. Things can get tough at home or at school. And even sports, which are supposed to be fun, can get us down when we strike out or kick our own goal or drive a tee shot into the water (if you're like me, you have those magical, "water-seeking" golf balls).

When those things happen, we need a friendly boost. Something to get our heads up. To encourage us. To help us remember that we're pretty special.

Way to Go!

And one more thing. When you're out on the field trying to help your team, and you do something right, what does the coach call what you did? She might say, "Hey, 'heads up' play out there. Way to go!" When you make a "heads up" play on the pitch or the field or the course or the court—it means you are paying attention and doing all the right things. Wouldn't it be great to get a "Heads up!" call from God? Kind of reminds me of the promise that someday we can look forward to being in heaven and hearing God say, "Well done!"

It's my hope and prayer that *Heads Up!* will help you toward that goal. If you like sports as much as I do, you enjoy reading a lot of stories about Christian athletes and how they handle life. And as a bonus, you'll find out a whole bunch of information about making yourself a better athlete—stuff I learned as a player in Little League, high school, and college, or things I learned in my years as a high school teacher and coach.

But beyond all that, as a fellow believer in Jesus Christ, my main goal for you is to grow closer to God as you read.

So, keep your head up—and your eyes focused on Jesus Christ.

> Consider it pure joy, my brothers
> and sisters, whenever you face trials
> of many kinds.
>
> James 1:2

PLAY BOOK ASSIGNMENT: READ JAMES 1:1–8

The Worst Thing

This is going to be a little hard to believe, but quarterback Drew Brees once called his move from the San Diego Chargers "the worst thing that has happened to me in my life."

Brees was drafted by the Chargers after his college years at Purdue, so San Diego is where he began his NFL career. He liked living in San Diego (who doesn't?), and he and his wife, Brittany, had started to do a lot of good deeds for the people in Southern California.

But then he hurt his shoulder. Even Drew himself knew it was a bad injury, calling it "potentially career-ending," but he was confident he could recover enough to help the Chargers.

The folks who ran the Chargers, though, did not agree.

So they let him go. Brees signed a contract to play football for the New Orleans Saints.

Here he was—moving from sunny, majestic Southern California to a town that had been pretty much destroyed by a hurricane. The team's stadium, the Superdome, was a mess. And the team wasn't much better.

However, Drew Brees taught us all something. As a Christian who wants to live for God, he knew what he had to do. He realized that God had something in mind for him—and he needed to do his best for his new team.

"God wouldn't let me face it if I couldn't handle it," he said.

With a positive attitude to guide his play and with a lot of faith in God to give him courage, Brees did everything he could to turn New Orleans around. Five years after he left San Diego, he took the New Orleans Saints to their first Super Bowl—and won.

A city that needed some good news and a team that had been called the "Aints" for much of their career suddenly were on top of the world.

What do you do when the worst thing happens to you?

Did you know that Jesus' brother has some advice for you on this? James, Jesus' half brother, said this: "Consider it pure joy ... whenever you face trials of many kinds."

And another Bible person, Paul, showed us how to make the best of some really bad situations. He was threatened with stoning. He was thrown in jail. He was shipwrecked. Yet he said that we should be content no matter what happens.

When the worst thing happens to you, talk to God. Tell him that you trust him. Tell him about your problems. Keep in mind that "God works for the good of those who love him" (Romans 8:28).

After Drew Brees led the Saints to a Super Bowl victory, *Sports Illustrated* named him the 2010 Sportsman of the Year. In describing him in an article in that magazine, the writer quoted Brees as saying, "My empowering word is faith."

Does your faith in God give you power? When bad things happen, trust the Lord and see what happens.

On the Chalkboard

When bad things happen to God's people, he knows how to turn them into good things.

Speaking of Injuries

The shoulder injury Drew Brees suffered while in San Diego was not his first major injury. While in high school, he blew out a knee. Instead of quitting, he worked his way through that injury so he could play college football.

Sports Stuff

One day when Brees was a college freshman, he was standing on the sidelines in practice with two other freshmen quarterbacks. The coach was frustrated with his older quarterbacks, so he looked over at the three freshmen. "Give me one of those guys!" he said. Brees stepped up and ran out on the field. He was ready for his big chance. Are you practicing hard enough so that when your coach calls on you, you will be ready? Don't get left behind. Be ready.

What has been the worst thing that has happened to you? Although you can't see the future, are you willing to "ask God" (James 1:5) for help?

Offer your bodies as a living sacrifices holy
and pleasing to God—this is your true
and proper worship.

Romans 12:1

PLAY BOOK ASSIGNMENT: READ 1 CORINTHIANS 12:1–7

Give It Up for the Coach

What are these students thinking?

It's six o'clock in the morning, and a bunch of swimmers are standing there at the pool, ready to jump in. Is this a polar bear swim or something?

No, it's the high school swim team, and the shivering students are getting ready for practice. While you're curled up under the blankets, dreaming about getting a good grade in math (dream on), these guys and girls are jumping into that water and swimming their legs off.

Let's say it gets to be 7:30 and they're still swimming. Their muscles ache. Their fingers are all shriveled up. And they know they've got a whole day of classes ahead. Just when they think it's over, the coach yells, "Ok, team, give me ten more laps."

And you know what? Even though they'd rather eat raw fish than swim another stroke, they do it. They flail those tired arms, and they splash their way wearily through those extra laps.

That's because athletes are "living sacrifices." When they show up for practice, they are saying, "Hey, Coach, do with me what you want. Work me. Teach me. Yell at me. Wear me out. I'm yours." They give themselves up for the team.

Are they crazy? What makes them do this?

They realize it's the only way they can be any good. You don't think the University of Connecticut women's basketball team won a gazillion games in a row by sitting in front of a big-screen TV eating French fries and Facebooking their friends, do you? No, they worked, sweated, strained, grunted, and groaned. They gave it up for Gino Auriemma, their coach. When he said, "Jump!" they asked, "How high?"

That's the kind of thing the apostle Paul is talking about in Romans 12:1. He's saying that we should say to God, "Here I am. I'm giving it all up for you."

Do you think you could do that for God? Could you ever say, "God, do with me what you want. Send me to Iceland if you want to. I'll do whatever it takes to give my life to you." That's a true living sacrifice.

Look at what else Paul said. He called giving ourselves up to God our "true and proper worship." That makes it ten times better than any sacrifice you will ever give a coach. You have to respect your coach and listen to him or her, but you're sure not going to worship that person. When we give God our lives, we are telling him, "You are worth worshiping."

He is, don't you think?

On the Chalkboard

Every part of me that I keep for myself is something God can't use.

Speaking of Going All Out

At the Wimbledon tennis championships in 2010, John Isner and Nicolas Mahut played the longest tennis match ever. Isner won after eleven hours and five minutes of play. In fact, their tennis match was played over three different days. The score of the final set was 70–68. In tennis, that score is usually something like 6–4. Now, that's giving it up!

Sports Stuff

What did I do today to make myself a better athlete? The best athletes always look for ways to make themselves better. Should I start running or doing push-ups or sit-ups? If I'm not able to do that kind of stuff, what can I start doing today to better myself in some other area of my life?

Instant Replay

What is one thing I can sacrifice, or give up, for God?

May the Lord direct your hearts
into God's love and Christ's perseverance.

2 Thessalonians 3:5

PLAY BOOK ASSIGNMENT:
READ 2 THESSALONIANS 3:1 – 5

God Loves You!

Imagine being an Olympic gold medal winner. Really. Think about it for a minute. What in the world must it feel like to realize that millions of people know who you are and that you are the very best person on the planet in your sport?

Does it feel good to imagine that?

Then what was wrong with Kelly Clark?

In 2002, she became the first American female to win the gold medal in Olympic snowboarding. She should have been on top of the world.

Famous. Rich. Popular.

And empty.

That's how she felt. In fact, she said that she was feeling that "if I didn't wake up tomorrow, I was fine with that. I didn't think anybody would care if I didn't wake up tomorrow. If this was what life was, then I was done with life."

Winning at sports is great, but it does not always lead to happiness.

Kelly was a champion in sports—but she was not doing very well at life.

But guess what helped her? She overheard someone talking to a friend who had lost her skateboarding competition. The person talking to the losing athlete said, "It's all right. God still loves you."

A light went on in Kelly's mind. *Maybe God loves me*, she thought.

She asked the person she had overheard to explain what she meant by her comment. The girl told her about Jesus and that she could have a relationship with God through him.

Kelly soon became a Christian and found out that no matter what happens in life—good or bad—she could make it through because she knew that God loves her.

Maybe you feel a little like Kelly. Lots of problems. Lots of trouble. And nobody really cares.

Keep this in mind. "It's all right. God still loves you."

That's the best news you'll ever hear.

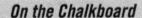

On the Chalkboard

No life is empty when Jesus fills it with his love.

Speaking of Snowboarding

Snowboarding has been a part of the Olympics since 1998. In the first four Olympics with snowboarding (1998, 2002, 2006, 2010), the US won nineteen medals out of a possible sixty.

Sports Stuff

If you have never snowboarded before, beware. It's not an easy skill to learn. One of the most difficult things for a beginner to get used to is being strapped to the snowboard. Also, you need to learn how to climb up an incline, you need to know how to stop, and you need to learn how to get onto the chair lift. Snowboarding is hard to learn, but for those who learn it is great fun.

Instant Replay

Ok, do you ever just sit there and think about the fact that God loves you? How does this love compare to the ways your parents love you?

In everything set them an example by doing what is good.

Titus 2:7

PLAY BOOK ASSIGNMENT: READ 1 CORINTHIANS 10:31 – 11:1

Tell a Teammate

If you pay attention to the NBA, you might have heard that Chris Paul and Stephen Curry have had some pretty good free throw numbers. But they weren't the best. That label belongs to Mark Price, the best free throw shooter in NBA history. When he finished his career in 1997, he retired with a career percentage of .904. This meant that for every one hundred free throws he took during the season, he made ninety of them.

But that wasn't the greatest thing he did as a player in the NBA. No, the best thing he ever did was to live such an impressive life that one of his teammates became a Christian because of it.

While a member of the Cleveland Cavaliers, Price had a teammate named Craig Ehlo. Ehlo and Price became friends. The more Craig watched Mark, the more he noticed that there was something really good about him (besides his shooting ability). Finally, Mark and his wife, Laura, asked Craig and his wife, Jani, to visit their house. That evening, Mark said, "Craig, if you were to die tonight, do you know if you would go to heaven?"

Because Craig trusted Mark, he took the question seriously, and that night he became a Christian. He prayed to put his faith in Jesus Christ.

Do you think your example can make a difference to others? Are friends who don't know Jesus like you do watching to see what kind of person you are? You might think they just want to know if you can hit a baseball or catch a football or shoot free throws. But more importantly, they are watching to see if what you say about being a Christian is the real deal.

Think about all the things you do with your friends throughout a day. You sit in class with them. You play ball with them. You talk on the phone with them. You hang out at each other's house. You ride bikes together. How many times during all of those hours together do you think about whether or not you are being a good example? It's not an easy thing to do.

That's why you have to ask God to help you be a good example. Not a Goody Two-shoes who tells everyone how righteous he or she is. Not a person who goes around telling everyone how bad they are. Just a dependable friend who keeps doing what is right.

Like Mark Price, be a good example. That's more effective than a 90 percent shooting average.

> **On the Chalkboard**
>
> **The best thing you can do for a friend is to introduce him or her to your Best Friend.**

Speaking of Excellence

In 2006, Deb Remmerde of Northwestern College in Orange City, Iowa, made 133 straight free throws during the regular season. That is the all-time record for any basketball player at any level. One time she made 485 straight free throws at practice.

Sports Stuff

What is the secret to good free throw shooting? Three things: balance, shooting position, and release. Keep your legs about shoulder-width apart and bend your knees for balance. Get finger pad control of the ball (don't let it touch the heel of your hand); bring it to the U-position (upper arm parallel to the floor, forearm straight up and down, and hand pulled back parallel to upper arm). Then release with a flick of the wrist as the arm is extended and as your legs straighten. Your index finger should be pointing toward the basket in your follow-through.

Instant Replay

If my friends were looking at me for an example, would they see Jesus in the way I act? Why or why not?

Jesus answered, "I am the way
and the truth and the life. No one comes
to the Father except through me."

John 14:6

**PLAY BOOK ASSIGNMENT:
READ JOHN 3:1–16**

Which Way?

Did you ever shoot at the other team's basket during a basketball game? That would be pretty embarrassing. But think of how embarrassing it would be to run a football all the way to the goal line—the wrong way!

In the Rose Bowl!

Talk about going from glory to goat in five seconds flat!

It happened a long time ago. Before YouTube. Before ESPN. Before television. Maybe before radio. It was January 1, 1929, and the University of California was playing Georgia Tech in the huge Rose Bowl game in Pasadena, California. Roy Riegels of UC grabbed a Tech fumble and took off for all he was worth.

After all, this was the biggest bowl game in college football at the time, and he had a chance to make history. So he ran. And ran. And ran.

All the while, his teammates were running after him, trying to flag him down.

Roy was running toward the wrong goal line.

Finally, just before he would have carried the ball across for a Georgia Tech touchdown, one of his teammates tackled him. On the next play, California was sacked in the end zone for a safety—giving two points to Georgia Tech and UC lost the game 8–7.

Ever since then, Roy Riegels has been known as Wrong Way Roy.

Did you ever think about whether you are going the right way? In life, that is. It happens to a lot of kids. Read this verse, and think about what it means: "There is a way that appears to be right, but in the end it leads to death" (Proverbs 14:12). In other words, people can think they are headed God's way only to discover that "Oops!" that wasn't it.

The right way to go is the way that Jesus says to go.

Here's what he said: "I am the way and the truth and the life. No one comes to the Father except through me" (John 14:6). That means that if you want to get to heaven, you need to put your faith in Jesus Christ.

Roy Riegels was sincere. He was running his hardest. The nearer he got to the goal line, the more convinced he was that he was headed in the right direction. He was doing his best and running his hardest. But he ran his team to a defeat.

Remember Wrong Way Roy and learn. Make sure you are going the right way—Jesus' way.

> ### On the Chalkboard
>
> **The wrong way is always the long way.**

Sports History Note

On January 1, 1902, the first Rose Bowl game was played. In that game, played in Tournament Park in Southern California, Michigan beat Stanford 49–0. The game is now played in Pasadena, California, in Rose Bowl Stadium, which was built in 1922.

Sports Stuff

Being prepared is the most important part of being a good athlete. To help yourself be prepared for when you'll get into the game, study the way a favorite athlete conducts himself. How does he or she respond in tough situations? How does he or she get ready for every play? If you pay attention to really good athletes now, you'll learn great lessons for when you get to higher levels of play.

Instant Replay

Do I know for sure I'm on my way to heaven? If not, who can I talk to about it?

was that day. He probably expected her to hold his hand and say, "Yes, Harry. You are right. How wise you are."

She didn't do anything of the kind. She looked over at her sweaty husband-to-be and said to him, "If you don't run, you can't win."

If the expression, "Well, duh!" had been popular back then, that would have worked too. Her statement was brilliant, yet simple.

Instead of quitting because of a small setback, she was telling him to go for it! You can't win if you don't try.

Harry listened to his lady and proceeded to go out on the track and win the Olympic gold in the 100-meter race. And he set an Olympic record too.

Often we want to be successful at being the kind of person God wants us to be, but we mess up. Then we decide to give up. We stop before God has a chance to help us do what he wants us to do.

Peter ran into that problem out on the Sea of Galilee. He was having a bad night fishing and was ready to quit. Then Jesus gave him a pointer, and he netted more fish than he could handle. Just think what he would have missed if he had quit.

Ok, what does God want you to do? Better start working on it. You can't get it done by just sitting there.

On the Chalkboard

If at first you don't succeed, it might be because you didn't try at all.

Speaking of the 1924 Olympics

Another runner in the 1924 Games was Eric Liddell. He refused to run a heat for the 100 meters on a Sunday, because he felt it would not honor God. This forced him to withdraw from the 100-meter dash, his best race. He then registered for the 400-meter run, in which he not only won but broke the existing Olympic record. His story is told in a movie called *Chariots of Fire*. You might check with your parents about watching it. After the Olympics, Liddell became a missionary to China. If you would like to read more about his journey, check out his biography, *Pure Gold*.

Sports Stuff

List three sports skills you know you need to improve on (dribbling a soccer ball, shooting layups, scooping a lacrosse ball — something like that). In the next two weeks, repeat this skill at least one hundred times a day in order to improve.

Instant Replay

Last week I failed at _____, and I was afraid to give it another try until now. Tomorrow I will be successful at it.

A man leaves his father and mother
and is united to his wife.

Genesis 2:24

PLAY BOOK ASSIGNMENT:
READ GENESIS 2:18–24

Music and Hockey

Most of the time, we think of professional athletes as being famous. And when they get married—the spouse moves from being someone no one has heard of to being famous because he or she is married to a pro.

But that's not quite the way it worked when NHL hockey player Mike Fisher got married between the 2009–2010 and 2010–2011 seasons. In his case, he got even more famous when he took his vows. That's because he married singer Carrie Underwood.

Suddenly two different kinds of fans had someone new to cheer for. If you like music, you probably already knew about

Carrie, who went from being an *American Idol* champion to becoming a superstar in the recording industry. And if you like hockey, you probably knew about Fisher, who spent many years playing for the Ottawa Senators.

Either way, you've got to like Carrie and Mike. They are a great example of the importance of marriage done the right way.

It's pretty clear that at your age marriage is not a hot topic. But at your age, you should be developing an attitude toward this great arrangement God designed. He first told us about it in Genesis 2—right at the beginning of the Bible—so it must be important. Look at Genesis 2:18–24 to see his instructions.

In today's world, you will find out that many people don't think marriage is very important. But it is important, and the Bible makes that clear.

Listen to what Mike said when writer Dave Pond interviewed him for *Sharing the Victory* magazine: "I'd just been patient, waiting for God to bring the right person into my life, and He provided. And being married is incredible. To have someone there to share your faith and your life with has been awesome. God is the reason Carrie and I are together, and we want to honor Him in every way we can."

And for her part, Carrie says of her husband, "He makes me a better person."

You need to begin now to consider how sacred and important marriage is. It is God's design for families—his way of making sure children are brought up to know and love God.

As you grow older, look for people like Mike and Carrie—Christians who desire to please God with their lives and who want to use God's plan for marriage as a way to serve him.

Hockey Note

One thing young hockey players sometimes have to do is move away from home as teenagers to play junior hockey. Mike Fisher was just seventeen when he did that, playing for Sudbury, Ontario, which is a couple of hundred miles from Fisher's family home in Peterborough, Ontario. Fisher says, "It was tough moving away. I didn't have any Christian friends on the team, and I didn't live with a Christian family." He had to be strong in his faith at an early age, and he was.

Sports Stuff

When you are young and just learning to play hockey (or other sports), is it important to be absolutely driven to be the best? Someone asked Mike Fisher what his best advice for young hockey stars of the future was, and he said simply, "Don't put too much pressure on yourself." Sure it's important to practice your skills, but you should enjoy playing. If you are good enough to move to the next level, you will be discovered. But don't make your life miserable in the process. "Have fun," Mike says. After all, it's just a game.

34

Instant Replay

What have I observed about marriage? What are some important principles for me to keep in mind as I grow up and think
about marriage?

Be strong and courageous. Do not be afraid;
do not be discouraged, for the LORD your
God will be with you wherever you go.

Joshua 1:9

PLAY BOOK ASSIGNMENT:
READ JOSHUA 1:1–9

It's Ok to Be Different

Some people have a hard time accepting Tim Tebow.

The guy is a little different from most other football players—in a good way though.

For instance, when Tim was playing college football at the University of Florida, where he won the Heisman Trophy as the best player in the country, he did something that caused the NCAA to create a brand-new rule.

Because Tebow is a strong Christian who likes to tell people about his faith, he started putting Bible references on the eye black under his eyes. (Some athletes wear that on their cheekbones to cut down on glare.) Anyway, soon there were pictures all over the Internet of Tebow's eye black messages from the Bible. In fact, one source reported that he got more than 100 million hits from people searching the Net to see what his messages said.

Among the verses he put on the eye black were John 3:16, Mark 8:36, and John 16:33.

For some reason, the people who run college football—the NCAA—decided to put a stop to that, and after Tebow was done at Florida they made a rule that players couldn't do that anymore.

They couldn't accept Tim Tebow's strong faith, apparently.

Also when Tebow was in college, he worked with a Christian ministry to produce an advertisement during the Super Bowl. The message was simple: His mom, who had been sick when she was pregnant with Tim, wanted to say that she was glad she had Tim and that life is precious.

A whole bunch of people complained about the ad (mostly people who hadn't seen it). Again, they couldn't accept Tim Tebow and his message.

Have you ever felt that other kids don't accept you—that they disagree with you about important things in life? Things like your faith?

When that happens, don't back down. If you are sure that what you are doing is honoring God (check with some adults about this), do what Tebow does. He stays strong, and he sticks to his faith.

It takes courage to do what might stand out for God when so many others are telling you to just go with the flow. But that's what God promised Joshua in Joshua 1:9. It's what Tebow demonstrated, and it's what can help you too.

When people don't like you because of your faith, remember that Jesus went all the way to the cross for you.

Sports Note

When Tim Tebow was drafted into the NFL in 2010, his Denver Broncos jersey immediately became the number one best-selling NFL shirt.

Sports Stuff

Tim Tebow was homeschooled by his mother. But his parents figured out that they could homeschool him and still have him play sports for his local high school. If you are homeschooled, ask your parents to help you find ways to participate on sports teams and experience the thrill of competition.

Instant Replay

What is the most important thing I can tell my friends? What if they don't like it? How can I make sure I lead people to Jesus and not away from him?

Anxiety weighs down the heart,

but a kind word cheers it up.

Proverbs 12:25

PLAY BOOK ASSIGNMENT: READ 1 TIMOTHY 3:6–10

Way to Go!

Do you know anyone who runs marathons? My brother has run them. He has even run in the Boston Marathon, which is the most famous one in the world. To him, it was the highlight of his running career. To me, it would be 26 miles and 385 yards of self-inflicted torture. Why, I used to think, would anybody, or in the case of the Boston Marathon, thousands of anybodies, run that far? For fun.

Wouldn't it be easier just to light fire to your shoes and whack yourself in the leg with a ball bat? Wouldn't that create the same end result?

Well, I've learned some things that have changed my thinking. I began to find out a little more about running long distances when my daughter and my son began running cross-country in high school. I discovered, for one thing, that people who run cross-country get a lot of encouragement. From everybody.

Have you ever been to a race—either a cross-country race or a marathon? It is so very different from the sports I'm used to—basketball, baseball, and football.

At ball games, fans yell at people, for the most part. "Hey, Number 10. Can't you dribble any better than that?" Or "Yo, Ref! Did you miss that foul on purpose or are you blind?"

At running events, fans yell for people. "Nice job, Mike! Way to run!" "Go, Rachel! You're doin' great!"

For some reason, a major part of running sports is that people go to the events to help the runners feel good about what they are doing. Some go to hand out water. Others just cheer. But no one goes and hollers, "Hey, Number 1395. My grandmother runs better than that!" So, one reason people run, I guess, is because other people like to shout encouraging things to them.

When it comes to how you treat your friends, your parents, and your classmates, are you like a cross-country fan or a ball game fan? Are you encouraging them or making them feel like day-old roadkill? Do you make positive comments that build people up or do you say negative, nasty things?

Look at the encouraging report Paul gave in 1 Thessalonians 3. Imagine how good this report made everyone—Paul, Timothy, and the people in Thessalonica—feel.

If saying "Way to go!" helps people run twenty-six miles, maybe telling a friend "You are special!" will help make her day.

Maybe if handing out a cup of water to a thirsty runner helps him run faster, imagine what you can do for someone in your class by doing something good for him or her.

On the Chalkboard

A word of encouragement speaks volumes about the kind of person you are.

Sports History Note

The first marathon was run in 1896 at the first Olympic Games of the modern era. (The last Olympics before that were held in AD 393.) The original distance was twenty-four miles, which was the distance a Greek messenger, named Pheidippides, ran in 490 BC from the Plain of Marathon to Athens, Greece, to tell his people that the Greeks had defeated the Persian army. The current distance of 26 miles 385 yards was agreed upon in 1924. Have you seen little stickers on the back of car windows that says, "26.3"? The driver or someone in that family is a marathoner: he or she runs 26.3 miles.

Sports Stuff

How far can you run? You might surprise yourself. Why not map out some distances in your neighborhood (half mile, mile, mile and a half) and test yourself. It's great exercise, and you might end up being a cross-country star. One goal is to run 3.1

miles, or 5K. That's the distance for high school cross-country. Want a goal for running a 5K? Try less than twenty-five minutes.

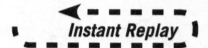

Instant Replay

Would I consider myself an encourager or a criticizer? Who can I encourage today?

The testing of your faith
develops perseverance.

James 1:3

PLAY BOOK ASSIGNMENT:
READ 2 TIMOTHY 2:1–3

Don't You Ever Win?

Did you know that there is an American athlete who has competed in the Olympics in three different events?

We all know about the people who are really good in one sport: Michael Phelps in swimming; Usain Bolt in running; Dwight Howard in men's basketball. But one woman has been in the Olympics four times in three different sports.

In 1996, she competed in swimming.

In 2000 and 2004, she competed in triathlon.

In 2008, she competed in the pentathlon.

You may not have heard of this woman, but she's one of the most remarkable athletes in Olympic history. Her name is Sheila Taormina.

Sheila had tried out for the 1992 Olympics but didn't make the team. And even her selection to the 1996 team was not easy. In fact, she was the last person to make the squad. And she was allowed to compete in the 4 x 200-meter swimming race only because someone else had been disqualified. But when she swam in 1996, she and her teammates captured the gold medal.

What makes Sheila truly remarkable, though, is her attitude toward life after she won the gold medal. Suddenly she was famous, and people all across the country wanted to see her and hear her speak. So she tried to make everyone happy. Anytime a group called to ask her to come to their event, she did.

And she took her gold medal with her. As she would tell her story, she would let the people in the audience handle that precious disk. She would do this even when she spoke in elementary schools. More than once, kids would drop or in some other way mistreat her prize possession. Sheila would just go on telling her stories.

Part of the story she told her listeners was the difficulty she had in making the US swim team. Sheila would tell of all the times she didn't qualify or all the times she didn't win—trying to let the kids know that it is ok to fail as long as you keep trying.

One time, as Sheila told her story, a little girl began to cry. Noticing this, Sheila put her arm around her and said, "Did I say something to upset you?"

With tears on her face and her big eyes turned toward Sheila, the little girl sniffed and said, "Didn't you ever win?"

You know what? Losing is sad. It's not easy to keep going when you don't get what you want.

But we can learn from Sheila. Physically, she wouldn't quit. And spiritually neither should we. God wants us to be tough when things are hard. Paul reminds us in Psalm 46 that even in times of trouble, "God is our refuge and our strength" and our "ever-present help" (v. 1).

Let's say you're struggling to read your Bible every day. If you miss a couple of days, don't quit. Start again. Or maybe you have a friend who isn't a Christian, and you want to witness to him or her. But then you slip and say something you shouldn't, and you feel like you've let God down. Paul gave you the answer. He said, "Be strong in the grace that is in Christ Jesus" (2 Timothy 2:1). It's not you who has to be strong. Depend on Jesus' strength.

Sometimes you might look at yourself and say, "Don't you ever win?" Just look back and say, "Jesus and I can do anything." Then go for the victory.

On the Chalkboard

You and Jesus are a winning combination.

Sports History Note

If you have trouble swimming from one side of the pool to the other, it'll be hard to believe what Gustave Brickner did. The Pennsylvania native, who kept track of how much he swam in a lifetime, covered 38,512 miles of water in his fifty-nine years of swimming.

Sports Stuff

Sheila is an example of an athlete who uses cross-training as a way to get better. Could cross-training (a little bit of several training routines instead of a lot of just one) help you with your favorite sport?

Instant Replay

Do I feel like a winner or a loser? If a loser, how can Jesus help me?

I love those who love me, and those who
seek me find me.

Proverbs 8:17

PLAY BOOK ASSIGNMENT:
READ DEUTERONOMY 10:12–21

Who's First?

Here's the perfect sport for you: triathlon.

Think about it. You like to ride a bike, don't you? And during the summer, you love to swim, right? Well, there is that little thing about running, but hey, you run to the fridge all the time during the commercials, so how bad can this be? Triathlon is a sport that combines all three of those really fun ways to exercise: swim, bike, run.

One of the best women's triathletes in the world is a woman named Barb Lindquist. She lives in Wyoming, and she loved training for this sport. She got so good at it that she ran for the US in the Olympics.

As a follower of Jesus Christ, Barb uses her fame as a great athlete to tell others about her Savior. And she tries to keep the most important things in her life in the order in which they should be.

Here's how things should be, according to Barb:

First priority: God
Second priority: her husband, Loren
Third priority: her sport, triathlon

She has a pretty good checklist for making sure she's doing things right. If any of these things start getting out of whack—for instance, if she puts running before God—she knows it's time to do some rearranging.

The best time to start developing this kind of priority list is right now. When you are young. When you have a lot fewer things to keep in order.

One day, you'll have a car, a spouse, a house, a job, money, friends, responsibilities at church, and other stuff. These things will all beg for your attention. It'll be really easy to end up having God be about number eight on your list.

So now, when your life is a little simpler and you have fewer things in the way, why not make it a point to put God at the top. Here's your own checklist:

1. Did I talk to God this morning before I talked to anyone else?
2. Did I ask God to help me throughout the day?
3. Did I look at God's message to me in the Bible, or did I have a bunch of other things that were more important?
4. Did I let anyone else know that God is important in my life?

Reviewing the items on your checklist may help you remember to fear the Lord, walk in all his ways, love him, and serve him (see Deuteronomy 10:12). It'll help you keep in mind who's first.

On the Chalkboard

For a relationship with God that will last, put him first.

Sports History Note

The sport of triathlon began in 1978 when two men challenged each other to a contest of 2.4 miles swimming, 112 miles biking, and 26 miles 385 yards running. The event attracted fifteen athletes, twelve of whom made it to the finish line. Four years later, the race had 580 competitors and gained extensive television coverage on *ABC's Wide World of Sports*. In all, it is estimated that between 200,000 and 250,000 triathletes compete each year in the United States.

Sports Stuff

Mom says, "You need to do some running and get into shape." Before you take off, remember this tip: It is always best to warm up a little before doing your stretching exercises. Running while your muscles are cold could lead to muscle tears.

◄ Instant Replay

Some wear a WWJD or PUSH bracelet to remind themselves of the importance of God in their lives. What do I plan to do?

> Above all else, guard your heart.
>
> Proverbs 4:23

PLAY BOOK ASSIGNMENT: READ EPHESIANS 5:1–11

Be Your Own Goalie!

Imagine playing hockey without a goalkeeper.

Once in a while it happens. At the end of some hockey games, a team that is behind will pull its goalie off the ice and put in another offensive player so they have a better chance to score a goal.

And sometimes when that happens, it backfires. Instead of the team with the extra man scoring, the team with the open net will send one across the ice and watch it slide untouched into the net. It's an empty netter, and it counts just as much as the one Jeff Carter got for the Philadelphia Flyers in game five of the 2010 Stanley Cup finals against Chicago. (Well, maybe not quite as much, since it's not for the Stanley Cup. But it's still a goal.)

Did you know it's possible to live your life with an empty net? It can happen when we don't know how to stop bad influences from sneaking into our lives—when we let them in just like a Sidney Crosby slap shot flying into the back of an unattended net.

That's why you need to strap on the pads and learn to play goalie. Not on the hockey ice, but in your life. You need to stand your ground against any kind of influence that might damage you.

For instance, when you hear someone start to tell a dirty story or when you get the urge to go to a forbidden website that you know is wrong, you need to guard the goal. You need to guard your heart, as the writer of Proverbs said. Every day, there are dozens of ways you can fill your heart with things that will harm you, so it's important to protect yourself.

The apostle Paul said we should imitate God. And one thing we know for sure about God is that he hates sin. Just like a hockey goalkeeper will do anything he can to stop that hated puck from getting into his net, so we have to protect our heart from anything that will separate us from God.

How are your goalkeeping skills?

On the Chalkboard

You can't stop sin by pretending it's ok; you have to hate it.

Sports History Note

In 2003, goalie Brian Boucher of the Phoenix Coyotes shut out the Coyotes' opponents for 332 straight minutes. His string of shutout hockey extended across parts of five games. It began in 2003 and ended in 2004.

Sports Stuff

When we talk about goaltenders, we're talking defense. Sometimes, young athletes don't like to talk about, or play, defense. The glory is in scoring, they think. But keep in mind that you can win a lot of points with a coach if you show him or her that you are willing to play good defense. Study good defenders in your sport and watch how they get the edge. No one wins without a good defense. Someday, maybe you can be the key to your team's defense.

Instant Replay

A goalie has gloves, pads, and a stick to protect the goal. What are my tools? How often do I use them?

Go and make disciples of all nations.

Matthew 28:19

PLAY BOOK ASSIGNMENT:
READ MATTHEW 28:16–20

Shouts or Whispers?

In 2007, the best soccer player in the world was a guy named Ricardo Izecson dos Santos Leite. But you can call him Kaká. He was voted the FIFA World Player of the Year and the FIFPro World Player of the Year.

This Brazilian-born star took the world of soccer by storm, and he earned praise from everyone who saw him play both in his home country and in Europe in the UEFA Champions League. He played for Milan, and he led them to championships before signing with Real Madrid. One year he even made *TIME* magazine's list of one hundred most influential people in the world.

But there's something else really cool about Kaká.

He is not afraid to tell people that there is something more important in his life than soccer.

He displays this priority whenever he and his team win a big championship game. He removes his team jersey to reveal a T-shirt that says "I belong to Jesus" or some other similar saying.

This is a loud and clear message. Kaká is not afraid to "shout" about his faith in this way.

Most athletes—even Christians—are not that brave. Many believers who compete in the world of sports prefer to whisper. Maybe they make some kind of gesture that no one really understands—like pointing to the sky. Or they might say, "Yeah, I go to church."

But not many athletes—and not many of us—are willing to tell the whole world about our love for Jesus the way Kaká does.

Maybe we need to listen to Jesus. He said, "Go and make disciples of all nations."

It's kind of hard to tell people about Jesus if all we do is whisper.

We all need to learn from Kaká—not just about soccer but also about being willing to make a statement about our faith.

Does anyone else know about your faith, or are you just whispering so no one can hear you?

On the Chalkboard

What good is Good News if we keep it to ourselves?

More about Kaká

As Brazilian football (soccer) star Kaká was growing up, he also enjoyed playing tennis, which he continued to play until he was fifteen. As a professional athlete, he has made his mark as someone who enjoys helping people in need. In fact, in 2004, at the age of twenty-two, he was selected by the United Nations' World Food Programme as its youngest ambassador ever. Also, he performed on his wife Caroline's first album of gospel music, *Presente de Deus*.

Sports Stuff

Do you play soccer? If so, did you ever set a goal (no pun intended) to try at least fifty shots on goal a day? Or to see if you can dribble a ball in the air for three minutes? Or to practice heading for five minutes a day? Set some goals, and see if you don't get better soon.

Instant Replay

Do I have a friend who shares my faith? How does that make a difference in my life?

What is your life? You are a mist that
appears for a little while and then vanishes.

James 4:14

PLAY BOOK ASSIGNMENT:
READ 2 CORINTHIANS 5:16–6:2

How Much Time Is Left?

Did you know that the World Cup of Soccer was played in the United States in 1994? The US made a bid to get the games back for 2022, but lost out to Qatar (look it up; it's in the Middle East). But back in 1994, the first game for the United States in the World Cup of Soccer was held at the Pontiac Silverdome, which was then the home of the Detroit Lions.

My family and I were at the Silverdome for an exciting game between the US team and Switzerland. As the game accelerated toward the final minutes, the score was tied at 2–2. Of course, the US fans were screaming and yelling for the Americans to put one more goal in the net as the teams frantically tried to move the ball.

Finally, the clocks in the Silverdome reached the ninety-minute mark. But the game didn't stop. The teams played on, as the referee on the field became the only person in the stadium who knew how much time was left. He had kept track of all injury and substitution time-outs, and he alone knew if there were two minutes left or five.

It was weird as a fan to sit there and not know if there was time for the US to score. Those were some tense minutes as the teams battled without knowing when the game would be over.

Finally, the ref blew his whistle, and the game ended at 2–2.

Life is like that soccer rule. There is only one Person who knows when our final whistle will blow and we will have to account for ourselves before God.

As a young person, you probably don't think much about dying. You're enjoying life too much. And besides, only really old people die, right?

Sadly, that's not true. Eight years after we were at that soccer game, one of my children, Melissa, was killed in a car accident. She didn't give much thought to dying; she was just a kid. But she had to be ready to meet God. There is nothing in this life that guarantees that you have any longer than a typical "extra time" period in soccer. Our lives are totally in God's hands.

The Bible says that our lives are kind of like a mist that is here one minute and—poof!—gone the next. In that little "mist" time, God asks us to commit our lives to him through Jesus Christ.

It's not any fun to think about the fact that we don't know if we will be here tomorrow, but it's important. God wants each of us to be ready to meet him. He wants us to make sure we have a personal relationship with him through faith in Jesus Christ.

And only God knows when time is up. Are you ready?

Sports History Note

The men's World Cup of Soccer has been contested since 1930. It has been held in Uruguay, Italy, France, Brazil, Switzerland, Sweden, Chile, England, Mexico, West Germany, Argentina, Spain, the United States, South Korea and Japan, and South Africa. Russia and Qatar are scheduled to host future World Cup events.

Sports Stuff

If you want to be ready at the end of a soccer match to take advantage of "stoppage time," you have to be in shape. You may have already played ninety minutes, and the game goes on. That's why it is important to work harder at conditioning than anyone else. Some soccer players don't take conditioning seriously, either before the season or during practice. If you want an advantage over everyone else, then train harder than everyone else. That will also help you overcome weak spots in your game.

Instant Replay

Do I know for sure that I have put my faith in Jesus Christ?

Prepare your minds for action.

1 Peter 1:13 (NIrV)

PLAY BOOK ASSIGNMENT: READ 1 PETER 1:13–21

What Are You Going to Do?

There's a runner on first and second. There is one out. The batter is left-handed, and he doesn't run very fast. Your team is ahead by one run in the last inning. It's a home game.

Your pitcher has the ball, getting ready to pitch. You are standing at shortstop with your hands on your knees.

What are you thinking about? How nice your uniform looks? What Mom is cooking for supper? What new computer game you want to buy? How blue the sky is? What it's going to be like to go swimming after the game? What you're going to feel like when you become a college All-American?

It better not be any of those things.

You're supposed to be deciding what you're going to do if the ball is hit to you. Or what you do if it goes to a teammate.

One of the most important principles in baseball or softball is to know ahead of time what you are going to do when the play begins. Every time your pitcher throws the ball, you're supposed to know already what you're going to do in any situation that might come up. Why? Because once the ball is in play again, you won't have time to make a lot of decisions.

Now let's leave the game behind and talk about life in the real world. Same principle applies. The key to success is to think ahead of time about all the possible situations. Then, when stuff happens, you're ready.

Peter reminds us to prepare our minds for action.

For instance, you're talking to a friend and he says, "My dad says God doesn't exist."

Or you're at the mall and the person you're with says, "Look at this shirt. I think I can get it out of here without paying."

Or you're at church and one of your leaders says, "Would you be willing to read a verse and talk about it next week for our class?"

Or you're walking home from a friend's house and a guy walks by, shoves some drugs in your hand, and says, "Here, kid. Try this."

Do you think you're ready for these situations?

Once the ball is hit to you, it's too late to come up with a plan. Prepare your mind for action.

On the Chalkboard

Failing to plan is planning to fail.

Sports History Note

There was little time for indecision on August 30, 1916. On that day two teams from the North Carolina League (a minor league) played a nine-inning baseball game in thirty-one minutes. It seems the visiting team from Winston-Salem didn't want to miss its train, so the manager asked the home team, Asheville, if they could speed things up. The game began at 1:28 and was over at 1:59.

Sports Stuff

One way to help yourself prepare is to keep a notebook of situations in your sport. You can jot down thoughts as you watch the pros play, or you can keep notes of what coaches tell you in whatever league you play in. For instance, if you play baseball, notice what major league teams do in bunt situations or in double-play situations. If you are really good on your computer, you can even make charts of game situations. It'll make the games more fun to watch, and you'll begin to understand the game better.

Instant Replay

What possible situation worries me? How can I prepare?

In the beginning God created the heavens
and the earth.

Genesis 1:1

PLAY BOOK ASSIGNMENT:
READ GENESIS 1

Who Invented Baseball?

Back in the mid-1800s, people began playing a game called "Base Ball." It started mostly in the eastern part of the United States before it spread west and then around the world.

There is some disagreement, though, about who invented the game. Some say it came from a game called "Rounders" that was played in England. Others say it was cooked up by Abner Doubleday. Still others claim it was created by Alexander Cartwright.

Although it's not clear who first came up with the concept, it's clear that someone did. The game did not just happen randomly. A bunch of people didn't just show up on a vacant lot one day to find pieces of wood that had become bats and hunks of leather and rubber and string that had developed into baseballs. They didn't find a field that was accidentally laid out with bases 90 feet apart and with a pitcher's mound 60 feet 6 inches from home plate.

No, there was a designer, or several designers, behind it all.

Now let's think about something a lot bigger than a baseball field. Let's think about the universe.

Nobody created it. It just happened. And out of the deadness of this universe, suddenly things started appearing on earth. Things without life in them all of a sudden sprang to life. They just developed life on their own. Of course, they weren't much. Just little, one-celled things. But they started changing into other things, somehow. They didn't have eyes, but they developed them over time. They didn't have ears, but they soon came along too. Then some of them made the jump from little, one-celled things to fish or something. And eventually some of them jumped out onto land. Their gills changed in a mysterious way to lungs. And some of them dropped fins and grew feet.

On and on the story goes. Unbelievable, isn't it?

But people believe it.

Baseball was invented; it didn't just appear.

The universe was created; it didn't just appear. God, who has existed forever, made the entire universe. He flung the stars light-years apart. He put the earth in the exact place it needed to be to support life (check it out; the earth has to be right where it is and have just the right temperatures). And God made earth a place of beauty. Then, to top it off, he made all living things, including us—each (species) after their own kind.

Ever think about how great God is because he made the world? We honor people all the time for what they invented or discovered or developed. We still remember the inventor of basketball, James Naismith, more than one hundred years later. Thomas Edison, who gave us electric lighting and other things, has several museums in his honor. We even honor people for coming up with things like Snuggies®.

But what about God? He created the whole world and everyone in it.

That ought to make us want to praise him and thank him and worship him. Our Creator-God is awesome!

On the Chalkboard

God's handprints cannot be erased from his creation.

Sports History Note

There are references to "base ball" in the 1700s, long before the game was said to have been invented by either Alexander Cartwright or Abner Doubleday. But it began to be popular in about 1850 or so. The first game on record was played in 1846 in New York.

Sports Stuff

Did you ever try to invent a new game? You might want to think about trying that. Remember, James Naismith invented basketball by using a volleyball in a different way. And his hoops were peach baskets. So, you can use existing items from other sports to create your own contest. Then get some friends together and try it.

Instant Replay

What is the most amazing fact about creation? Should I spend a few minutes thanking God for all he made?

But when you pray, go into your room,
close the door and pray to your Father,
who is unseen.

Matthew 6:6

PLAY BOOK ASSIGNMENT:
READ MATTHEW 14:22-23;
MARK 1:35

A Place to Pray

If your church looked like a shower room, would you go?

For many professional athletes, that's exactly where they go to pray.

Most pro basketball, baseball, and football teams have a chaplain who meets with the players at least once a week, usually on Sunday, to pray and study the Bible. They meet wherever they can find a quiet space away from the noise of a team preparing for a game. And sometimes, the best place to meet is in the shower room. Nobody goes in there before the game.

As the season wears on, the players look forward to getting together for chapel, because they know they will have a special place to pray. No matter whether it's a training room, a coach's office, or the shower room, this prayer sanctuary helps the players stay in touch with God.

Do you have a special place in your house where you can pray? Imagine how nice it would be to have a place where you go every day to meet with God. Maybe there's a spare room in the basement where people seldom go. Or perhaps your dad's workbench in the garage. Or it could be your own bedroom.

Make it someplace where there is no TV, no computer, no cell phones, no Wii. Put a Bible there and a pad of paper on which you can write down prayer requests. And put up an Off Limits sign when you go there so everyone else in the family knows to leave you alone with God.

When Jesus wanted some special time alone with God, he sometimes went into the hills near Jerusalem. That was his refuge where he could have heart-to-heart talks with the Father. You may not be able to have a place as majestic as a Judean mountain, but that's ok. Jesus suggested that you "go into your room, close the door and pray" (Matthew 6:6). You can definitely do that!

Developing a prayer place could make a big difference in your relationship with God. You'll find yourself looking forward to getting together with him.

It may not be a shower room or a mountain, but think about finding a place to pray.

On the Chalkboard

When you get alone to pray with God, you are not alone.

Sports Note

Baseball was the first pro sport to have regular chapel services. Baseball Chapel was started by a sportswriter named Watson (Waddy) Spoelstra. (His grandson Erik was the coach of the Miami Heat when LeBron James arrived there in 2010.) In the 1960s, Waddy went to the commissioner of baseball, Bowie Kuhn, and asked for permission to have Sunday services with the players who wanted to attend. Now there are chapel programs in the NFL, the NBA, the WNBA, the NHL, and Major League Baseball.

Sports Stuff

If you have a favorite player and you'd like to write to him or her, send your letter in care of the team for which that athlete plays. You may have to do a little research, but if you go to the team's website, you usually can find an address. If you want a reply or an autograph, send a self-addressed, stamped envelope.

Instant Replay

Ok, where is my prayer room going to be? In the next week, I vow to use the room at least five times.

A gentle answer turns away wrath, but a
harsh word stirs up anger.

Proverbs 15:1

PLAY BOOK ASSIGNMENT:
READ MATTHEW 5:38-42

Base-Brawl

When you think of home runs and baseball, you usually think
of Ryan Howard or Albert Pujols. But what Kim Braatz did is
pretty important too when it comes to home runs.

Of course, Kim's effort didn't get her on the cover of *Sports
Illustrated*, and it didn't turn a baseball into a million-dollar
piece of memorabilia, but it's a big deal.

Kim hit the first over-the-fence home run for a team of
women baseball players who played against men. She played for
a team called the Silver Bullets, which was made up of some
really talented women baseball players.

On July 16, 1996, while playing in Cape Cod, Massachusetts, Braatz belted a low fastball over the 315-foot sign in left field to make her mark on history.

That wasn't the only thing Kim did on the baseball field that year that made history. The second thing, however, is something she's not quite as proud of. Well, actually, she's not proud of it at all.

In a different game that season, Kim found herself in the middle of the first fight in women's-men's pro baseball. It seems that the pitcher of an opposing team nailed her with a pitch. That would have been ok, but then he laughed at her as she made her way to first base.

Bad idea. Kim thought her honor as a baseball player was at stake, so she headed out to the mound to settle the score with the pitcher. A fight followed, and Braatz had her second first of the season.

Later, Kim, a strong Christian woman, had second thoughts about the fight. She knew that a lot of people looked up to her because of her faith, and she felt she had let them down. "I shouldn't have done that," she finally concluded. "I should have turned the other cheek." She decided that Jesus was not happy with the way she responded.

What she did by reacting incorrectly is no different from what we do when we respond with harsh words or mean comments to something someone says to us. The big difference in Kim's situation was that her act was witnessed by a lot of people, including reporters who sent her story around the country.

Kim learned from her mistake, and she realizes now how harmful anger can be.

Do you struggle with anger? Do you get mad easily if your parents tell you no? Do you fly into a rage if your brother or sister looks at you the wrong way? Do you yell at your teammates if they don't do what you think they should?

Here are a couple of verses that can really help. But you can't just read these and forget about them. You need to write them on a card and put them where you will see them. On your bulletin board in your room. In your locker at school. On the bottom of the bill of your baseball cap. Wherever they can help remind you of God's method of handling anger.

The first is: "A gentle answer turns away wrath" (Proverbs 15:1). You can make sure a little problem doesn't get big by answering people calmly and kindly. The second is the one Kim referred to: "If anyone slaps you on the right cheek, turn to them the other cheek also" (Matthew 5:39). That means you let some stuff go. You don't fight back. Both suggest that if we want to please God, we'll seek to avoid trouble with our responses, not make it worse.

Be careful not to turn someone else's comment into your own version of base-brawl.

On the Chalkboard

If you want to get angry at something, get angry at sin.

Sports Stuff

You don't have to be huge to hit home runs. Kim is just 5' 7" tall. The first secret is in good forearm strength. That was the situation with Hank Aaron, who hit 755 home runs for the Braves and Brewers back in the 1950s through the 1970s. He had great forearms. Another secret that will help you hit a baseball or softball farther is bat speed. So, strengthen those forearms and increase the speed of your bat as it moves through the strike zone.

Instant Replay

I have a problem with anger. I don't have a problem with anger.

Which sentence describes me? If I do, what am I going to do to stop it from causing me problems?

I rejoiced with those who said to me,

"Let us go to the house of the LORD."

Psalm 122:1

PLAY BOOK ASSIGNMENT:
READ HEBREWS 10:24–26

Maya's Mind-set

Once in a while a basketball player comes along who is far and away the best in the land. Someone who is so talented and adds so much to a team that he or she sets a new standard of excellence. One such player is Maya Moore, who led the way for the University of Connecticut when the Huskies broke UCLA's consecutive win streak of eighty-eight straight college basketball wins in 2010.

So good is Maya that one rival coach said, "She's on track to become the greatest player ever."

But she is more than just a skilled basketball player. As a student, she got straight A's. And as a Christian, she went against the grain of many college students by staying strong in her faith and staying connected to her home church. Statistically, a large number of college-age young men and women reject the faith during that time in their lives. One study showed that 52 percent of Christian students who go to a public university will not consider themselves Christians by the time they graduate.

Maya is not like that. In fact, she does something that points out how important her faith and her church are to her. On Sunday, while at UConn, she would grab a notebook and sit down at her computer, go online, and watch her home church's live streaming service. When her pastor would give his sermon, she would be right there—800 miles away—but taking notes on what he said.

"My faith is the core of who I am," Maya told a reporter from the *Atlanta-Journal Constitution*. "I know my faith has helped me keep that mind-set of being humble, to appreciate every day."

Can you learn from Maya's mind-set? Are you eager to learn more about Jesus Christ by going to Sunday school or trying to listen closely to your pastor's messages? Do you listen to Christian music? Do you read stuff that comes from Christian sources?

When you are at school, there are all kinds of influences around you that could drive you away from your faith and from God. There's a passage in the New Testament that says, "Let us consider how we may spur one another on toward love and good deeds, not giving up meeting together, as some are in the habit of doing" (Hebrews 10:24–25).

It reminds us that getting together with other believers is essential. We need the encouragement, the instruction, the fellowship, and the friendship of others as we face daily challenges to our faith.

Do you have Maya's mind-set? Make your church a vital part of your life. It's one of the best ways to stay close to Jesus.

On the Chalkboard

When someone says it's time for church say, "Let's go," not "Oh, no."

Honoring Maya

Here are some of the awards Maya Moore won at Connecticut: 2008 National Freshman of the Year; 2009 Big East Player of the Year; 2009 Big East Tournament Most Outstanding Performer; 2009 First Team All-American; 2009 National Player of the Year; 2010 NCAA Final Four Most Outstanding Player. In the game in which Connecticut won for the eighty-ninth straight time to break UCLA's men's record of eighty-eight consecutive victories, Moore scored forty-one points as UConn beat Florida State.

Sports Stuff

Let's talk about dunking a basketball. Maya first put one down when she was sixteen years old. You have to have two essential ingredients to dunk. First, you have to have some height (although players like Spud Webb, 5' 7", and Nate Robinson, 5' 9", could dunk), and second, you have to have some hops. You have to be able to jump. The first thing can't be taught;

the second one can. There are a number of drills that you can do to increase your vertical leap. You need to increase the power in your calves and quads (look it up). Wall sits help with this. Also, toe raises help your calves. Also, practice jumping while using light ankle weights. Jump over short objects side to side. Or pick a spot on the wall and jump to touch it with a series of reps. You may be too young to dunk now, but if you keep at it as you grow, perhaps someday you can have the thrill of throwing one down.

Instant Replay

How do I get most of my Bible knowledge? Can I see how valuable it is to attend church with other believers who can encourage me?

This happened that we might not rely on ourselves but on God.

2 Corinthians 1:9

PLAY BOOK ASSIGNMENT: READ 2 CORINTHIANS 1:2–11

Double Trouble

Want to hear a sad story?

Greg Oden was a rookie for the Portland Trail Blazers in 2007. Before he could play in his first preseason game for the Blazers, he suffered a fracture in his right knee. The injury meant he would have to have surgery and miss his entire rookie season. Then he could begin to get ready for the 2008 season.

Which is exactly what Oden did.

He played parts of the 2008–2009 season and parts of the 2009–2010 season, suffering knee injuries both years.

Then, just as the 2010–2011 season began, it was discovered his old 2007 injury was back. He would again have to have microsurgery on his knee.

Talk about double trouble.

Let me guess. You've had trouble that seems just as bad to you as what happened to Greg. You've lost your homework, had your best friend move away, failed to make the soccer team, and found out that your cat is going to die. All in the same week. And then things got worse.

Why is it that really bad things happen to someone as really nice as you? Where is God when you have more trouble than a kid should have? Is he not paying attention? Is he on vacation?

It might help to understand a couple of things about problems.

First, just because you are a Christian doesn't mean you won't have any trouble. Look at what happened to the guy many think was the greatest Christian ever: Paul. He was thrown in jail, beaten, shipwrecked, jeered, and mocked. And he even asked God three times to take a specific problem away, but God didn't do it (2 Corinthians 12:7–10). Second, God has a reason for the trouble we go through. In 1 Peter, we are reminded that we suffer these trials so God can be praised and honored.

Here's the most important thing to remember: Our Christian life is not about us. It's easy to think that God is there to serve us. But it's the other way around. We are here to serve him, and if it takes trials for him to get the honor he deserves, then that's the way it should be.

Speaking of Injuries

Matthew Stafford was one of those guys who couldn't catch a break when he started his career. He was drafted by the Detroit Lions in 2009. He became a rookie starting quarterback for the Lions. In the fourth game of the year, he suffered a knee injury and was out for a few games. Then he separated his shoulder in November and was done for the season. In the first game of the 2010 season, he separated his shoulder again in the first game. He came back several weeks later and had the Lions ahead of the New York Jets when he separated his shoulder again to end his 2010 season. Two years. Four major injuries. Ouch.

Sports Stuff

Some injuries in sports can't be avoided. Others can be. For instance, if you're into skateboarding or rollerblading, be sure to wear a helmet, knee pads, wrist guards, and elbow pads. It may not seem cool, but it's not especially "cool" to have a concussion, either. In sports like baseball, football, and basketball, warming up properly and then stretching your muscles may help avoid injuries (as well as wearing mouth gear). In baseball, using the right technique for throwing will help you preserve your arm. Take a little extra time to make sure you don't bring on injuries that can be avoided.

What is my greatest problem right now? How can I make sure God gets the glory as I struggle through this?

The Lord disciplines the one he loves.

Hebrews 12:6

PLAY BOOK ASSIGNMENT:
READ HEBREWS 12:1—11

Stop Yelling at Me!

Coaches come in all shapes, sizes, and styles. But what most kids are interested in when they begin a new sport is this: "Is my coach going to yell at me?"

Some coaches think the best way to get their point across is to YELL AT YOU REALLY LOUDLY SO YOU DON'T MISS WHAT THEY ARE SAYING!!!!! Those coaches aren't too much fun.

Others might not be quite so loud, yet they can throw some zingers your way that make your ears burn.

The next time you watch the NCAA men's and women's basketball tournaments, notice the coaches. There are some coaches who pace the sidelines looking like they are about to explode. Others are intense and serious but under control. Sometimes it's more fun to watch the coaches than the games.

Back in the 1970s, there was a basketball coach who some say was the greatest coach of all time. His name was John Wooden. He would sit calmly on the bench with a rolled-up program in his hands. He never yelled or screamed. He simply talked to his players, guiding them quietly through their game plans. His method worked. His team, UCLA, won ten NCAA titles.

No matter what style your coach displays, there will come times when he or she will have to point out some things to you that you are doing wrong. Your response will go a long way toward telling what kind of athlete you will be.

If you listen and learn, you'll get better. If you pout and refuse to learn, you'll never improve.

This old saying has helped a lot of young athletes: "The player who is never criticized is the one who should worry." In other words, if your coach never yells at you, it may be because he or she doesn't consider you a key part of the team. Coaches tend to spend the most time on players who will help the team.

Let's look at this idea in relation to your faith. God, like a coach, may find it necessary to discipline you. When he does, listen and learn. He knows what's ahead, and he knows just what you need.

On the Chalkboard

Learning from God takes listening to God.

Sports History Note

In his twenty-nine years of coaching on the college level, John Wooden compiled a record of 664 wins and just 162 losses. He coached one year at Indiana State (1947–1948) and twenty-eight years at UCLA (1949–1975). During all those years, he had just two technical fouls called on him by referees. John Wooden died in 2010 at the age of ninety-nine.

Sports Stuff

Being criticized by a coach is never fun. However, you can help make the best of the situation. First, stop what you are doing and look your coach in the eye. Second, listen closely to what the coach says. Third, if you have to respond, don't do so in an argumentative way. Be respectful. Fourth, avoid trying to show the coach up after he or she has talked to you. Go out and try your best to correct your error.

Instant Replay

In what ways have I ever felt that God was guiding me to change what I was doing? Did I listen?

For the eyes of the LORD range throughout
the earth to strengthen those whose hearts
are fully committed to him.

2 Chronicles 16:9

PLAY BOOK ASSIGNMENT: READ PSALM 34:15—18

Tough Guy, Tough Talk

LaDainian Tomlinson is one tough guy.

For several years, he was the top running back in the NFL. He played for the San Diego Chargers before moving to New York to play for the Jets. You know he is tough because of the beating he had to take on every play as huge linemen did everything they could to bring him down.

But he was also a tender guy.

During his years with the Chargers, he was excited to find out that his wife, LaTorsha, was going to have a baby. Here was this big, strong guy with massive arms—eager to hold a tiny little baby girl and take care of her. "I'm going to give that child a lot of love. Just a lot of love," said LT as he waited for his baby girl to be born.

But then something horrible happened. The baby did not survive being born. She died, and LaDainian Tomlinson—tough guy—had to take care of his grieving wife. He had to cry with her and try to help her through their toughest time.

LT had to lean on his faith in Jesus Christ during this time.

A friend of his later described Tomlinson's strength during this time as something that was "developed by a life of faith." LaDainian was right there to comfort LaTorsha and help her during this tough time. She later said, "He sacrificed his own needs to stand up and be there for me."

Life can be hard sometimes.

Often, things at home can be really rough. Problems with parents. Or parents with problems.

Maybe you are struggling with tough stuff that happens outside your home. Perhaps someone you thought was your friend suddenly turns on you and talks mean about you behind your back.

Or perhaps school life is very difficult for you. While other kids are writing down answers to their math homework as fast as they can, you struggle to get through the first problems on the page.

Tough times can come in sports too. You don't make the team. Or if you do, you hardly get to play.

One thing to remember is that you are not alone. Many, many kids go through similar problems. Even the ones who seem to have it all together are probably hiding something that is bothering them.

But the most important thing to do is to take a hint from LT. Sometimes you forget that you're not in control. But God knows everything.

You never have to go through your tough times by yourself. God is watching, and he is "attentive to [our] cry" (Psalm 34:15).

And you know what? God's tougher than any problem you'll ever face.

> ### On the Chalkboard
>
> **There's nothing you are going through that God can't help you survive.**

Sports History Note

During his playing days, LaDainian Tomlinson set the following records: Most touchdowns in a single season (31), most rushing touchdowns (28), most points scored in a single season (186), and most 200-plus rushing games in a season (5).

Sports Stuff

Often star athletes have players they revered as kids. For LaDainian Tomlinson, the players he watched most closely were Emmitt Smith, Jim Brown, Barry Sanders, and Walter Payton. What are five techniques and characteristics you see in your sports hero that you can try to copy and practice?

Instant Replay

What is my toughest problem? Have I ever thought to talk to God about it and give it to him?

For just as we share abundantly in the
sufferings of Christ, so also our comfort
abounds through Christ.

2 Corinthians 1:5

PLAY BOOK ASSIGNMENT:
READ 1 PETER 2:19-23

Not Fair!

For a few years before becoming a writer, I was a high school
basketball coach. When I get together with some of my old
players, the conversation usually rolls around to a couple of bad
things that happened to our team.

One was the time we had a two-point lead with four seconds
left and a player on the other team hit a 3/4-court shot at the
buzzer to send the game into overtime (this was before three-
point shots), and we lost. The other frequently mentioned event
was when we were in the district semifinals and one of our players missed a game-winning layup at the buzzer. We lost that
game too.

We all can laugh now remembering how much it hurt to lose those games and how unfair it seemed. But those two losses don't compare with something else that happened when I coached.

One of my players died.

One day he was the happiest, friendliest, most energetic kid. The next day we were trying to cope with the word "cancer." About a year after we first found out that Keith was sick, six of my basketball players were pallbearers at his funeral.

Losing games was bad, but losing Keith was devastating. That's when you start to say, "It's not fair!"

What can you do when life isn't fair? Give up?

Never.

You talk to Jesus. Above anyone who ever lived on earth, Jesus knows what "Not fair!" means. After all, he left the unbelievable home he had in heaven to live as a poor carpenter's son in Israel. Then, when he grew up as the first perfect human ever, he was captured like a common criminal. He was beaten and mocked. Even his innocence couldn't protect him from being crucified.

Jesus Christ can help us with life's unfairness because he understands. He went through it for us, and he wants us to tell him our burdens. He trusted God when he faced unfairness, and he wants us to trust him when we run into the same problem.

Life seem unfair? Tell Jesus.

On the Chalkboard

The world may not be fair, but Christ's sacrifice makes it good.

Sports Stuff

Not all athletes who hear the word "cancer" from their doctors lose their lives. Lance Armstrong, a cyclist, was diagnosed with cancer. After treatment and recovery, he won the Tour de France, the most grueling bicycle race in the world. It pays to have a doctor look you over on a regular basis to make sure you have a clean bill of health.

Instant Replay

When I get down about something that I think shouldn't have happened, would it help to read about what Jesus went through for me?

Saul replied, "... you are only a young man."

1 Samuel 17:33

PLAY BOOK ASSIGNMENT:
READ 1 SAMUEL 17:32−50

Too Small?

Danny, Chad, and Avery all had a problem. They wanted to play sports, but they weren't big enough. People kept telling them to give it up, that they'd never make it, so they might as well stop trying.

There's probably something you'd like to do in life but you are too small or too tall or too young or too something. When you feel that way, it's easy to give up on your dreams, isn't it?

Think of what would have happened if David had said he was too small to fight Goliath.

Or if God would have let Moses refuse to lead the people of Israel because he wasn't a good speaker.

Or if Caleb had thought it was impossible to take the Promised Land because he was too old.

Everybody has something that is not perfect about him or her. But do you think anyone ever got anywhere by worrying about what he couldn't do or what was wrong with her?

Let's put God into this situation (well, he's already in it, but you know what I mean). He has a little bit to do with the way you are. After all, he made you.

And he made you for a reason. Just the way you are.

God wants to use you just as you are. He wants to use the special characteristics he gave you.

Which brings us back to Danny, Chad, and Avery. Although they kept hearing that they were too small, they kept trying. They kept trusting that God would honor them for using the skill he had given them. That's how Danny Woodhead had an outstanding small college career at Chadron State before becoming a key player for the New England Patriots, how Chad Curtis got to a two-time World Champion with the New York Yankees, and how Avery Johnson got a ring as a part of the NBA champion San Antonio Spurs.

Too small? Not in God's eyes.

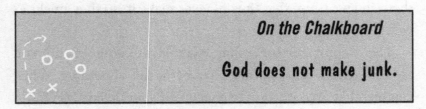

On the Chalkboard

God does not make junk.

Speaking of Short

The shortest baseball player ever was twenty-six-year-old Eddie Gaedel. He was just 3' 7" tall when he pinch-hit for the St. Louis Cardinals in a 1951 game against the Detroit Tigers. Wearing number 1/8, he walked on four pitches. It was his only major league at bat.

Sports Stuff

To overcome a weak area, the best thing to do is to get better in some other area. If you want to be a basketball player but think you are too short, then become the best ball handler you can be. And never give up working on your shot. If you want to be in baseball, but you know you aren't very good, then begin now to prepare for something like broadcasting, sportswriting, or working in a team office. Spend time on your interests and what you do well, and stop worrying about what you can't do well.

Instant Replay

What do I think my biggest problem is? How can God use me and my questionable characteristic?

Let your light shine before others.

Matthew 5:16

PLAY BOOK ASSIGNMENT:
READ MATTHEW 5:13−16

You and Armando

Imagine that one day you were in Armando Galarraga's shoes. You were pitching a baseball game, and suddenly everything came together for you. Maybe you were just an average pitcher who won a game now and then, but you lost more times than you won.

But on this magical day, everything turned out just right.

You got all three batters out in the first inning, and nobody thought anything about it. Same thing in the second inning.

No biggie. Anybody can get six straight batters out.

But then you do it again in the third. And the fourth.

Now people are starting to get nervous. You have a perfect game going, and even in your league that's pretty rare. You overhear your coaches talking and they say they don't think anyone has ever pitched a perfect game in your league.

You go out for the fifth inning, and now you are having trouble breathing. But you somehow keep getting the ball over, and the other team keeps popping up and grounding out.

Everybody knows what's going on now. The parents in the bleachers are all standing up and cheering when you walk back to the bench. A couple of girls look at you for the first time ever.

You sit alone on the bench and you are shaking all over. You can hardly remember your name anymore. But when it's time to walk out to the pitcher's rubber for the sixth and final inning with a 3–0 lead, you somehow do it.

The first batter gets hold of your first pitch and sends the ball to deep centerfield. Your good buddy Oliver takes off for it, leaps into the air, and catches it right before it would have gone over the fence.

Two to go.

The next guy, a lefty, strikes out on a pitch in the dirt. He must have been more nervous than you.

And then it's down to one guy. He swings at the first pitch and dribbles the ball to the right side of the infield. The first baseman goes over, grabs it, sets, and throws to you as you cover first.

It looks like the ball gets there first and you had your foot on the bag before the runner did, but apparently the umpire didn't see it that way. He spreads his hands out for a "safe" call.

Everybody comes unglued. Coaches, players, and fans alike are screaming at the umpire. He's just a kid. Probably 18. But he stands behind his call. You know he missed it, and everybody but the guy with the blue shirt on knows it too. Suddenly, you realized that your perfect game is gone.

So what do you do?

This happened to Armando Galarraga when he was pitching for the Detroit Tigers in 2010. On the last out of what would have been just the twenty-first perfect game in major league history—and that covered 135 years at the time—the umpire missed a call at first base. Galarraga took the throw from his first baseman Miguel Cabrera, and he stepped on first before the runner got there—but the umpire spread his arms out to signal safe.

What did Armando do?

He smiled. That's it. He smiled, gathered himself, and walked back to the mound to pitch to the next batter. He never complained. He didn't criticize the umpire.

He handled this disappointing situation so well and with such grace and class that the next day he was presented with a brand-new car for his dignity and for his great pitching performance.

And how could he handle this problem so well? His dad had taught him that at all times he needs to stay under control and keep his emotions in check.

In other words, he had learned ahead of time how to handle a problem and how to act when trouble comes.

Now it comes back to you. How do you handle things that don't go your way? At school? At home? In sports? Are you willing to control your emotions in bad situations as a testimony of God's faithfulness to you? When tough things happen, do you smile and shine Jesus' light on the situation?

That's the goal. Start practicing.

On the Chalkboard

The best reaction to a difficult situation is one that points to Jesus, not you.

Sports Stuff

Let's say you want to become a pitcher. Sometimes it helps to have a dad who can guide you and explain to you how to throw. That's what happened with Tim Lincecum, who won two Cy Young awards with the San Francisco Giants by the time he was twenty-five. But if you don't have a dad who knows how to turn you into a pitcher, you can work on your pitching by yourself. Read up on proper ways to pitch, and practice throwing to a friend. Don't try to throw curve balls but just try to build up your arm strength and learn to throw strikes. Control is a key issue when you are just getting started.

Speaking of Perfect Games

Just four days before Armando Galarraga pitched his near-perfect game, Roy Halladay of the Philadelphia Phillies pitched baseball's twentieth perfect game. A few weeks earlier, Dallas

Braden pitched one for Oakland. Then, in the playoffs that season, Halladay pitched a no-hitter.

Instant Replay

How do I usually handle things that don't go my way? What should I be asking God to help me with in those situations?

Get Mark and bring him with you.

2 Timothy 4:11

PLAY BOOK ASSIGNMENT:
READ ACTS 15:36–41

This Cut Hurts

Want to make a grown-up cry?

Find one who was cut from a sports team when he or she was younger, and then ask that person to tell you about it.

If you know much about former NBA star Michael Jordan, you know that he was once cut from a basketball team. Actually what happened was that Michael, who became one of the greatest players ever, tried out for the varsity and was told he would have to play on the junior varsity.

I know that can hurt, because it happened to my daughter one time. She was a high school sophomore who thought she had earned a shot at the varsity basketball team. When she was told she would have to spend one more year on JV, she was pretty upset. Tears and everything.

And I know it can hurt because when I was a senior in high school, I was cut from varsity. After playing from seventh grade through my junior year, I was told, "See ya." From the time I was twelve, my deepest desire was to be on that varsity-level team and to play in front of my friends. But the coach had other plans. Ouch! That still hurts.

So, how do you handle things when they hurt like that? What do you do when you are really, really feeling rejected? When you have to look up to see the curb?

There's a Bible character who got cut from the team one time. His name is John Mark, and he was cut from Paul's missionary team.

In Acts 15, you can read about the powwow between Paul and his partner Barnabas. They were talking about taking a trip to visit the Christians in some of the towns where they had preached earlier. Barnabas wanted to take John Mark with him, but Paul didn't. Paul said that John Mark had failed on an earlier mission, and he apparently didn't trust him.

Paul and Barnabas couldn't agree, so they split up. Barnabas took John Mark with him, and Paul went another direction.

That must have been embarrassing for John Mark. But you know what he did? He worked himself back into Paul's favor. In 2 Timothy 4:11, Paul said, "Get Mark and bring him with you, because he is helpful to me in my ministry."

Apparently, John Mark recovered from his disappointment and continued to work hard for God. Paul noticed it, and he let Mark rejoin the team.

We can learn a lot from Mark. His failure didn't stop him from doing great things for God.

On the Chalkboard

How you respond to rejection reveals how well you'll rebound from it.

Sports Stuff

Want to avoid being cut from the team? Know what coaches are looking for. Of course, they are first looking for some athletic ability. But beyond that, everything else is something you can do to make your chances better. Here are some key ways to impress the coach:

1. Have a great attitude.
2. Hustle all the time on the court or field.
3. Be a team player.
4. Listen closely to instructions and do exactly as you are told.
5. Learn the drills and perform them as designed.
6. Take the sport seriously.
7. Stay under control when things don't go your way.

Instant Replay

How have I been rejected recently? What can I do to follow Mark's example?

Live such good lives among the pagans that,

though they accuse you of doing wrong,

they may see your good deeds and glorify

God on the day he visits us.

1 Peter 2:12

PLAY BOOK ASSIGNMENT:
READ HEBREWS 12:1–15

Making an Impression

They should call it the "embarrassment card."

In soccer, when you do something really bad, the ref runs over to you, pulls a red card out of his or her pocket, and shoves it in your face. When you see that dreaded red, you are one sunk soccer player.

In front of your team, the other team, and everybody else who's standing or sitting around the sidelines watching, you have just been kicked out of the game. No warning. No chance to do better next time. It's simply "See ya later."

You get one of those, and your ears will glow like a sunburn on a hot August day. You know that you've done something really wrong, and you've just made a terrible impression on everybody there.

There's a team of professional soccer players who make it their goal to avoid getting any red cards. In fact, they don't even want yellow, which is a warning.

The team is the Charlotte Eagles of the United Soccer Leagues Second Division. This North Carolina squad is made up of Christian players, and they are trying to be a witness to others of their faith in Jesus Christ. Two of the players have been league MVP: Jacob Coggins (2004, 2005) and Dustin Swinehart (2008).

As Christians, they don't want to make that bad impression. "Our goal is to go through the season without getting any yellow and red cards," the Eagles' general manager Tom Engstrom said. "We want to be an example that you can have the highest level of sportsmanship and compete."

That's a great goal for all of us. Even if we're not playing pro soccer. Even if we're just playing a little one-on-one in the driveway. Or even if we're playing Scrabble in the family room.

Making a good impression by staying under control goes far beyond how you act on the soccer field. It also should show up in all kinds of situations. At school, when a friend says something bad about you, how do you respond? At church, when you don't get the recognition you thought you deserved for some good work you did, what's your reaction? At home, when your little brother "borrows" your iPod, how angry do you get?

Day after day you will face situations where people will be watching your actions to see if you are what you say you are. Would they red card you?

> ### On the Chalkboard
>
> **What we do speaks so loudly, people sometimes can't hear what we say.**

Male and Female Eagles

There is also a women's elite soccer team connected with the Charlotte Eagles. The Lady Eagles made the playoffs in each of their first ten seasons in the United Soccer Leagues' W-League.

Sports Stuff

Want to avoid getting a red card? Learn to know what the officials are looking for. Here's what they can give you a red card for doing: (a) committing an act of violence or a serious foul, (b) using foul or abusive language, (c) continuing to break the rules after a caution. Avoid those and you can avoid the embarrassment. And be a good witness.

Instant Replay

What are some things I know in my life are red card things — things I know I shouldn't do because they make the wrong impression on people who need to know Jesus?

As the deer pants for streams of water, so
my soul pants for you, my God.

Psalm 42:1

PLAY BOOK ASSIGNMENT:
READ JOHN 7:37—39

Thirsty?

You've just spent the last hour practicing your ball handling
and your shooting. You are hot and sweaty. What's the first
thing you do?

If you're like most athletes, you go for something to drink.

Watch any tennis match or any sports team. What do the
players do when there's a time-out? They reach for the water
bottle or the Gatorade or the Powerade or the Propel.

That's smart. The body loses a lot of liquids when we exercise, and the best way to get them back into the system is by
taking a nice, long swig of something wet.

Well, not just anything. Some things are better for you when you are thirsty than others. Water is best. Sports drinks are great. But a cola is not the best at that time. In fact, that kind of drink has a downside because of the caffeine in it. The important thing, though, is to get liquids into your system.

Did you know you can get spiritually thirsty too?

If it's been a few days since you've prayed or read the Bible or gone to church, you might be able to understand what that means. You don't really think about God much. You find it easy to think some thoughts you shouldn't think. You're thirsty.

In Psalm 42, you can see how David described being thirsty in that way. He said it's like a deer that can't wait to get to a stream and drink.

When that happens, instead of heading for the water bottle, head for Jesus. Listen to this invitation: "Let anyone who is thirsty come to me and drink. Whoever believes in me, as the Scripture has said, rivers of living water will flow from within them" (John 7:37–38).

When you turn to Jesus, he can give you peace, joy, contentment, love, understanding, hope, and answers to your problems.

Talk to Jesus. It's the coolest drink you'll ever take.

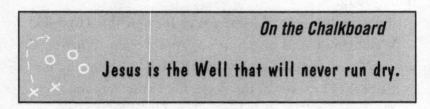

On the Chalkboard

Jesus is the Well that will never run dry.

Sports Stuff

What should you drink when you are playing sports? That depends on how long you are training. If you are competing for longer than an hour, then sports drinks can be helpful. They give you an energy boost and can help the body absorb fluid faster than water can. If you are training or competing for less that an hour, just use water. Another thing to do is to drink water two hours before you play so your body has enough fluids before you start.

Instant Replay

What makes me the thirstiest when I get away from it? Missing Bible reading? Not praying? Not being in church?

They went out and got into the boat,

but that night they caught nothing.

John 21:3

PLAY BOOK ASSIGNMENT:
READ JOHN 21:1–6

You Didn't Win. Now What?

Everybody has a failure story.

You know, when you missed the layup and your team lost by one. Or you kicked a soccer ball into the wrong goal. Or you got sick the day of the biggest game of your life. Or your team was supposed to win but didn't.

Aaaauuuugggggh! Don't you just hate that! Makes you want to dig a big hole to hide in.

So what happens next after you fail? After your favorite sport turns on you like an angry Rottweiler.

NFL quarterback Colt McCoy had one of those days when he was in college.

He was the quarterback for the Texas Longhorns, who had one of the best teams in the country. The Longhorns were so good that they earned a shot at winning the national championship in 2010.

The game started, and things immediately went bad for Colt and his teammates.

On the very first series of plays, an Alabama player tackled him and hurt his shoulder.

And it was his throwing shoulder, which is pretty bad news for a quarterback.

He was hurt so badly that he could not return to the game, and Texas lost to Alabama 37–21. It was a huge disappointment for Colt because it was his chance to lead his team to a national championship.

When he was asked what it meant to have to watch from the sidelines, he said, "I love this game. I have a passion for this game. I've done everything I can to contribute to this team. It's unfortunate I didn't get to contribute. I always give God the glory. I don't question why things happen the way they do."

Nobody likes to fail. It can ruin your whole day!

Sometimes when things don't go well, we get a little embarrassed because we don't want anyone to think we are losers.

But the best way to get over our losses is to realize that if we know Jesus Christ, he's the only person we have to really be concerned about. And we know he loves us more than we can ever imagine. We aren't alone. When we blow it or don't succeed even though we try really hard, Jesus will be right beside us, offering his peace.

Back in Peter's day, he failed big-time when he couldn't catch any fish. When Jesus found out about it, he helped Peter with his problem. Now, he won't always fill our nets with fish, so to speak, but he will always listen and provide his comfort and help.

You failed? Who hasn't? Turn it over to Jesus. Talk to him about it. See what he can do for you.

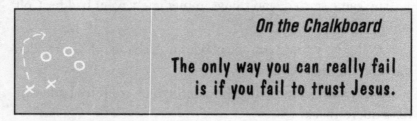

On the Chalkboard

The only way you can really fail is if you fail to trust Jesus.

Weird Football Fact

The oldest college football player was a guy named Tom Thompson. In 2009, he kicked an extra point for Austin College against Trinity University. He was sixty-one years old.

Sports Stuff

We've talked about the spiritual side of making mistakes in sports, what about the physical? What should you do when you make a mistake?

1. Don't blame someone else. Sure, there could have been a coach or another player involved, but it's up to you to admit your error.
2. Review the mistake. Sometimes, you can see a mistake on a videotape that Dad or Grandpa made of your

game. Although it's painful, look at it again to see what you did wrong.

3. Ask advice. Ask your coach or your mom or dad how you could have made the play right.

4. Practice. If you missed a putt, get out on the practice green and hit ten in a row of the same putt until you feel comfortable.

Instant Replay

What has been my biggest failure? Have I talked to Jesus about it and given it to him?

In all this you greatly rejoice,
though now for a little while you
may have had to suffer grief in all kinds
of trials, . . . [they] may result in praise.

1 Peter 1:6–7

PLAY BOOK ASSIGNMENT:
READ 1 PETER 1:3–9

A Mother's Death

Life isn't supposed to happen like it did for Hubert Davis when he was sixteen years old. It was all out of order. Your mother isn't supposed to die when you're still in high school. Mom is supposed to hang around long enough to watch you graduate from high school and go to college and get married and give her grandkids.

She's not supposed to get oral cancer and die when you're in the tenth grade.

So, when Ira Davis died as Hubert was just old enough to get his driver's license, Hubert was mad. Especially at God.

Sports History Note

Did you give me the five push-ups I asked for? Well, if you did, you are on your way to world record status. You need just 45,996 more to tie Charles Servizio's best-ever mark for push-ups. Servizio did 46,001 of them in one twenty-four-hour period. Ready? Down and up. Down and up. Down and up ...

Sports Stuff

If you are really into exercising, then you don't need this advice, but if not, here's a place to start. Why not make it your goal to put together a simple program of exercise. Start with as many push-ups as you can comfortably do. Same with sit-ups. And running. For the push-ups and sit-ups, add one each day. (Five today, six tomorrow, seven the next day. Just think, in one hundred years or so, you'll catch Charles Servizio!) With running, walk or run a little more each day until you can run an entire mile.

Instant Replay

How would I judge my spiritual fitness—a blob, an average Joe, a world-class fitness nut?

What can I do to improve?

> You know when I sit and when I rise; you
> perceive my thoughts from afar.
>
> Psalm 139:2

PLAY BOOK ASSIGNMENT:
READ JONAH 2

Oops!

Just in case you didn't know, $300 is way too much money to spend on a week's worth of laundry. It would be cheaper to throw your dirty clothes away and start all over.

That's why professional tennis player Tara Snyder was pretty upset. She was in Tokyo, Japan, to play in a tournament. While staying in a hotel, she sent some clothes out to have them cleaned. You've heard of the expression, "taken to the cleaners," haven't you? It means that someone tricked you and stole from you without your understanding that they were ripping you off.

Well, Tara got taken to the cleaners. The laundry people sent her clothes back. They were clean, all right. And she was cleaned out. The clothing bill was for $300.

"I didn't know what to do," Tara says, telling her story. "I prayed really hard and then went to see the manager of the hotel. I told him that I had no money to pay the laundry bill. The hotel took care of it." In other words, they paid Tara's bill.

"God was looking out for me!" Tara says.

Do you feel that God is looking out for you? It's easy to see how he can do that. In the Old Testament book of Psalms, in chapter 139, we are told that God knows when we sit and when we rise. He even knows our thoughts.

Because God knows so much about us, we know for sure that he is looking out for us.

Think about what happened with Jonah. He messed up a whole lot worse than Tara. She made an honest mistake, but Jonah did something wrong on purpose. But God was looking out for him anyway. After he got tossed into the water, he would have drowned if God hadn't sent the big fish to give him a three-day ride.

God has his eye on you. He cares deeply for everything that happens to you, and he wants what's best for you.

That's got to make you feel really special!

On the Chalkboard

There's no place we can go where God is not there.

Traveling Tennis Players

Want to travel and see the world? Be a tennis player. In one recent year, participants in the women's professional tennis tournament circuit played in the US, Russia, New Zealand, Australia, Tasmania, Japan, France, Jakarta, Germany, Italy, Wales, Spain, Scotland, England, Czech Republic, and Canada.

Sports Stuff

Tennis is one of those sports that you can play when you are young and carry it over to when you are, well, as old as your parents and beyond. If you aren't already a tennis player, why not get a racquet and start banging a few balls against a wall (not the garage door). It's a great time to learn a great game.

Instant Replay

How did God take care of me this week?

We put no stumbling block in anyone's path.

2 Corinthians 6:3

PLAY BOOK ASSIGNMENT:
READ 2 CORINTHIANS 6:3–10

What to Do with Pressure

"Hey, Mike! Let's skip practice today. It's too hot to play soccer. Let's ride our bikes over to McDonald's for a milkshake."

"We can't do that! We have a game tomorrow."

"Oh, come on, man. What's it going to hurt to miss one practice? We don't do anything the day before a game anyway."

Have you ever faced that kind of situation before? It's tough to make the right decision sometimes when someone your own age does this. In fact, pressure from a friend is probably the hardest to overcome.

You probably hate this term, but it's "peer pressure," and it can make you do almost anything.

NHL hockey player Shane Doan faced all kinds of pressure as a pro on the ice. But he learned early in his life that the best way to handle pressure is to let it make him a better person. While talking about some of the decisions he has to face as a Christian in the rough National Hockey League, he says that something he learned as a kid helps him even now.

"Peer pressure has never really bothered me that much," he said. "It almost makes me stronger."

He learned that as a kid growing up in Canada. His parents had a Christian camp there, and they expected Shane to "set an example" for the other kids at camp. Not only did he have to withstand peer pressure, he had to have a higher standard than the others.

As an adult playing for the Phoenix Coyotes, he realized that you can't get away from peer pressure. In fact, he discovered that the pressure was even greater because he began playing in the NHL as a teenager. He had to make decisions about how he would respond to things the older players on his team might suggest.

Let's go back to the story at the beginning. What is the big deal if you skip practice with the other kid? What does it hurt? Soccer's not that important, is it?

No, soccer isn't. But being trusted is. Here's how Shane says it: "I am scared of making mistakes, not just because I'm hurting myself, but others too. It's tough to make mistakes and then try to show God to people."

One of the best reasons to resist bad peer pressure is that giving in makes it very hard to witness to your friends. Why would they want to know God as you do if your life is no different from theirs?

On the Chalkboard

Getting away with something may cause a friend to get away from God.

Sports History Note

Players in the NHL regularly join the league before their twentieth birthday. But rarely are they discovered before they are teenagers. One player was, though. In 1960, some officials from the Boston Bruins went to see a game of youngsters. To their surprise, the best player on the ice was twelve years old. The officials discovered that the kid's name was Bobby Orr. Six years later, he signed with the Bruins and became one of the best players of all time.

Sports Stuff

One of the biggest controversies surrounding hockey and Christians is the fact that the sport is so rough. Some people wonder how a Christian can play a sport where hitting people with teeth-jarring checks are acceptable. Here's what Shane Doan says: "I have no problem with being on the ice and being very physical. David had the heart of a warrior, and the Bible says he was a man after God's own heart. I'm very competitive. I like to play a rough-and-tumble game." Doan was so well respected that he was the captain of the Phoenix Coyotes for several years.

Instant Replay

What are some peer-pressure decisions I have to make? How can I make them in a way that leads to a witness for Christ?

But in your hearts revere Christ as Lord.
Always be prepared to give an answer to
everyone who asks you to give the reason
for the hope that you have.

1 Peter 3:15

PLAY BOOK ASSIGNMENT:
READ 2 CORINTHIANS 5:14–20

Will They Listen?

"Nobody will listen to me. I'm just a kid."

If you have friends who aren't Christians, do you ever feel this way when you think about telling them about Jesus? It's ok, because most people your age feel that way from time to time.

It's not easy to talk to a friend about stuff like that when you're young.

But if it's something you might want to do, here's some advice from a former major league baseball player. His name is Sid Bream, and he used to play for the Atlanta Braves.

One year, he scored the most dramatic run of the entire season. It was the final game of the playoffs between the Braves and

124

the Pittsburgh Pirates. Winner goes to the World Series, loser goes home. The score was tied in the bottom of the ninth. Bream was on second. A teammate screamed a single into the outfield and Sid raced for home. The throw came in, he slid, and he was safe at home. The Braves won!

As important as that victory was, Bream considers his salvation a much more important victory. And he has the following advice for you if you want to witness to friends.

1. Earn your friend's respect. For a baseball player like Bream, that meant showing up, working hard, and helping the team.
2. Talk to God. You need God's help, guidance, and direction. "Prayer prepares your heart," Bream says.
3. Know what you're talking about. That's why you need to listen in church and read the Bible.
4. Be aware. "We are the light of Christ," Bream says. We need to be aware that we are God's witnesses.

This doesn't mean you have to be a preacher or something before you can witness. But if you're serious about helping your friends discover Christ, these suggestions might help.

Will they listen to you? If they are your friends, they will. And if you're prepared, you may just help them become "safe at home"!

On the Chalkboard

When your friends are ready for the gospel, be ready to give it to them.

Sports History Note

Sid Bream's team, the Atlanta Braves, went to the World Series five times during the 1990s. They won it in 1995. This was after having the worst record in their division in 1989. They played in baseball's postseason for fourteen years in a row—from 1991 through 2005. After Bream retired from baseball, he coached a minor league team during the summer of 2008, but he said he didn't want to keep doing that because it kept him away from his best friend: his wife, Michele.

Sports Stuff

The play at the plate on a ball from the outfield is one of the most exciting plays in baseball. One reason is that it involves so many people! The runner, the third base coach, the next batter (who signals to the runner to slide or not), the catcher, the outfielder who fields the ball, one or two infielders who are the cutoff people, the pitcher, who backs up the plate, and one or two umpires. As many as ten people are involved. And if there are other runners on base, there could be as many as thirteen people in on the play.

Instant Replay

Who of my friends would I like to try to witness to? How do I get ready to do that?

Live such good lives among the pagans that,
though they accuse you of doing wrong, they
may see your good deeds and glorify God.

1 Peter 2:12

PLAY BOOK ASSIGNMENT:
READ MATTHEW 5:13–16

Why Play?

Why do you play sports? Is it because your parents want you to? Is it because someday you want to play in one of the BAs: the WNBA or the NBA? Are you thinking you might get a college scholarship? Do you play just for fun? Do you play because your friends play, and you want to be with them?

There's nothing wrong with any of those reasons. As long as you have fun and don't take things too seriously too early, what can it hurt?

I'd like to suggest another reason to play.

This one comes from Keri Phebus, a professional tennis player. Keri played college tennis at UCLA, and she was very

Yes, the answer is *d*. Something else.

Here's what Paul said to do—no matter what: Give thanks.

When your dog gets sick and can't fetch any more: Give thanks.

When your little brother irritates you by running around yelling, "To infinity and beyond": Give thanks.

When you are having trouble understanding math: Give thanks.

See, the apostle Paul said, "Give thanks in all circumstances; for this is God's will for you in Christ Jesus" (1 Thessalonians 5:18). God is so good and so trustworthy that we can trust him no matter what. Somehow, what has happened—even if it stinks—is a reason to thank God because he can make something good out of it.

It's okay to ask God questions as you try to figure things out. David did a lot of that in the Psalms. But he always ended by praising God for his greatness.

Even if we have a flat tire, fail to make the team, or even suffer through a tragedy: Give thanks.

On the Chalkboard

Our thanks go to God for who he is — not just for what he does.

Sports Stuff

How did Dallas Clark get so good that he played for the Indianapolis Colts? He practiced the fundamentals of catching a football. Keep these keys in mind: 1. Keep your eye on the ball. 2. Extend your arms toward the ball as it is coming to you. 3. Form a triangle with your hands, palms facing up and away from your body. 4. As the ball comes into your hands, let it go halfway between your hands, then clamp down on it. 5. Tuck the ball into your body.

Instant Replay

What is the difference between praying to God and asking him some hard questions about what is happening and complaining to him?

I have learned to be content whatever the circumstances. I know what it is to be in need, and I know what it is to have plenty. I have learned the secret of being content in any and every situation.

Philippians 4:11–12

PLAY BOOK ASSIGNMENT: READ PHILIPPIANS 4:10–13

What's Wrong?

Each person has something about himself that is not perfect. Just look around at the kids in your class. Some kids have braces, which means somebody thought their teeth needed a little help in heading the right direction. Some have glasses, which means their eye doctor says their eyes aren't quite right. Others, well, you know what the problems are.

What's wrong with you? What difficulty do you have that you wish you didn't have to deal with every day?

Here's something that might help. It's from Jean Driscoll, a woman who won the Boston Marathon eight times in the wheelchair competition. She knows about having something wrong. Her legs don't work, so she gets around via her own set of wheels. Read how she handles what some would consider a big hassle.

"I look at my disability the way somebody might look at their glasses. That's the way I envision my chair. Somebody who wears glasses, that person puts those on in the morning, and then they forget about them the rest of the day. They don't go through the day thinking, 'Oh, another day with nearsightedness.' As for me, the first thing I look for in the morning is my chair. Once I'm in it, I forget about it."

What a great attitude! Driscoll, who is a Christian, is a great example of living out the verse that says, "I have learned to be content whatever the circumstances."

Now there's a challenge! If you can have the same kind of attitude that Paul (the writer of Philippians) has, then you can be happy even when things aren't right.

To be honest, Jean Driscoll didn't wake up one day when she was ten years old with the great attitude she has now. When she was your age, she was really, really upset with God for allowing the problems she has.

Jean always had a hard time keeping up with her sister and brother because even before she lost the use of her legs, she didn't get around as well as they did. She had a spinal problem when she was born, and she was never able to use her legs in a complete way. By the time she was a teenager, she wondered why God was picking on her.

Later, though, Jean trusted Jesus Christ as her Savior and she began to develop a really close relationship with him. That helped her trust him so much that today she can look at her disability this way.

Whatever challenges you face, turn it over to God. Then remember Jean and her wheelchair. It'll help you see that life is good despite the fact that you're not perfect.

> **On the Chalkboard**
>
> **The best state to live in is the state of contentment.**

Stuff about Jean

Jean Driscoll is a remarkable woman. Friendly, kind, intelligent. The kind of person who gets honored over and over. For instance, she has received honorary doctorates from two universities: the University of Rhode Island (1997) and the Massachusetts School of Law (2002). One unique honor was being named the Godmother of the Royal Caribbean Voyager Class Series ship called *Mariner of the Seas*. Her impact as a Christian athlete led the Fellowship of Christian Athletes to name her to its Hall of Champions in 2010.

Sports Stuff

Is there something you have to overcome to be a better player in your favorite sport? Use that problem to your advantage. Let's say you are a baseball player and you are afraid of the ball.

Admit that you are, then get in there and prove to yourself that it doesn't matter. Each time you stand in the batter's box and refuse to back off when the pitcher throws, you gain confidence. Soon, you'll be using that fear as a reason to get back in and stand your ground. Sometimes kids who are afraid have someone practice with tennis balls to help them not fear the pain of getting hit.

Instant Replay

What is something about myself that makes me discontent? How can I find a way to think about that in the way Jean Driscoll thinks about her disability?

And the boy Samuel continued to grow
in stature and in favor with the LORD
and with people.

1 Samuel 2:26

PLAY BOOK ASSIGNMENT:
READ 1 SAMUEL 2:18–26

When Am I Grown-Up?

How old are you?

Are you enjoying being that age? Are you looking forward to being a year older?

If you're like most kids your age, you're eager to be that next year older.

Here's another question. Are you pretty grown-up for your age? Most of the time, the answer is yes. No matter if someone is ten or eighteen, he or she thinks, *Yeah, I've got it together. I'm pretty mature.*

That's why parents and kids sometimes have little battles over stuff like clothes and rules and friends. It's one side telling the other that there's still some growing up to do.

Now what about growing up spiritually? Most of the time, you're not in as much of a hurry to make that happen. Maybe you're a little like Josh Hamilton, who was the Most Valuable Player in the American League in 2010. He was really slow to grow up—and it almost cost him his baseball career.

After Josh graduated from high school, he was selected as the top pick in the major league draft. That usually represents a straight line to the major leagues.

But Hamilton made some very immature decisions. He had not grown up.

He began using illegal drugs, and pretty soon his life was a mess. He not only couldn't play baseball, but he was barely able to stay alive.

Because he hadn't grown up and didn't make adult decisions, he was right on the edge of becoming a hopeless, homeless drug addict.

But he had people like his grandmother who didn't give up—who kept praying for him and who finally showed him how to trust Jesus as his Savior.

When he became a Christian, he realized that he needed to mature. He got married, stopped taking drugs, and got back into shape. Soon he was cranking home runs again and on the way to becoming a superstar.

Samuel must have been the kind of young man who, like Josh, knew he needed to grow up.

It wasn't his grandmother who helped him but the priest Eli. Samuel must have listened very closely to Eli, for he continued to grow up and be more mature, even though Eli's own sons didn't. They never did grow up, but Samuel became a very mature man of God.

Samuel is a great example of a person who learned from someone older how to follow God. Do you know anyone who could be an Eli for you, someone you could learn from?

So, you are you ready to grow up ... spiritually?

On the Chalkboard

Growing up spiritually is much more important than growing up physically.

Speaking of Being Young

The youngest major league baseball player of all time was Joe Nuxhall, who pitched for the Cincinnati Reds when he was just fifteen years old. Nuxhall, who was from a town near Cincinnati, pitched in just one game in 1944.

Sports Stuff

Sometimes when an athlete is really good, he or she ends up playing with kids much older. Like the freshman girl in high school who plays on the varsity basketball team. That usually happens either because the girl has grown up physically before others or because she worked really hard to get ahead of her classmates. Here's a concept that can help you if you want to get a head start on others your age. Think: Somewhere, someone my age is practicing. I will not let her work harder, practice longer, or improve more than I do. When I play against her, I will be ready.

How can I tell when I've been mature about something?

Whatever you do, work at it with all your
heart, as working for the Lord,
not for human masters.

Colossians 3:23

PLAY BOOK ASSIGNMENT:
READ PHILIPPIANS 3:12–21

Don't Quit!!

If you had a choice between flying a plane in the air force or playing football for the Dallas Cowboys, you'd probably pick ...

Tough choice: Either strap yourself into the cockpit of a plane that rips through the atmosphere at Mach 2 or strap on a helmet and play football for the most celebrated team in NFL history. (Girls can play this wishing game too, you know. There are women pilots, and lots of girls—including former soccer star Michelle Akers, who before playing for the US Soccer team in the World Cup, wanted to grow up to play for the Steelers— have football dreams.)

One person never had to make the choice between flying high and blocking low. He got to do both.

His name is Chad Hennings, and he played on the offensive line for the Cowboys in Super Bowls XXVII, XXVIII, and XXX (that's twenty-seven, twenty-eight, and thirty, if you're not up on your Roman numerals).

When Chad was in college, he went to the Air Force Academy. That meant that after he graduated, he was required to stay in the air force for several more years. For a player who was drafted by the NFL, that means only one thing—waiting.

While everyone else who was drafted signed fat contracts and spent their time battling it out in front of tens of thousands of people, Chad was stuck on some air force base somewhere. One of the things he did during that time was to fly the A–10 Warthog—a plane that carried supplies to people near Iraq.

Because of his great athletic talent, Chad might have been able to worm his way out of being in the service. But he didn't. He was taught by his parents when he was a kid that once you start something, you don't quit. And he wasn't about to quit on the US Air Force.

Eventually, after fulfilling his obligation, he was able to join the Cowboys and play in those Super Bowls. But when he was waiting in the air force, he didn't know that was going to happen.

How are you at sticking to a job you've been given? Do you get about a third of the way through an assignment and give up on it? Do you start writing a book report and stop after five minutes with terminal writer's cramp? Do you take so long to wash the dishes that the water is cold by the time you are finally done?

Speaking of Preparation

One year, Lou Whitaker, a second baseman for the Detroit Tigers in the '80s and '90s, was unprepared for the All-Star Game. For some reason, he showed up at the park for the game without his uniform. He had to borrow a uniform to play in the game.

Sports Stuff

When you have a game, it's important to prepare properly. One thing you must do is prepare your body by eating right— even the day before the game. Talk to a coach about what the right foods are for the day before and the day of a game. Next, make sure you get enough sleep the night before the game. Another thing you have to do is prepare mentally. Think about what you are supposed to do in the game, and even take yourself mentally through some situations. Then, make sure you are prepared with the right equipment. Almost everyone who plays sports has a horror story about forgetting his shoes or jersey. Have a checklist to make sure you don't forget anything.

Instant Replay

Who is one friend who I don't think is a Christian? How can I get this person's attention?

Lead a quiet life ... so that your daily life
may win the respect of outsiders.

1 Thessalonians 4:11–12

PLAY BOOK ASSIGNMENT:
READ 1 THESSALONIANS 4:7–12

Get Ready

You may not think so now, but someday little kids may look up to you as a role model. Just like you now look up to the stars on the varsity teams at your school or maybe to your favorite players on the college or pro team you cheer for. If you get better and better at your favorite sport, kids will think you are the best. They may even want you to autograph something.

Really. It could happen.

Not many of the top athletes in college or the pros knew when they were young how good they were going to be, and many probably never gave any thought to someday being role models.

But then they got to that position, and they were tested to see if they were ready.

One really good football player who has thought about this idea — and who has some advice for you — is quarterback Case Keenum. He led his University of Houston teammates to being the top offensive team in the country in 2009. He was on his way to a big 2010 season when he tore a ligament in his knee in the third game of the season.

He realized that as a Christian and a star football player, he had a big influence on kids. Here's what he said about it in *Sharing the Victory* magazine: "Being a football player, you have influence. I tell kids all the time that, no matter what, somebody is watching."

The apostle Paul had a suggestion for when people are watching us. He said, "Make it your ambition to lead a quiet life: You should mind your own business and work with your hands, just as we told you, so that your daily life may win the respect of outsiders" (1 Thessalonians 4:11 – 12).

That's a great idea to keep in mind. Even today, somebody is watching you compete. And how you handle yourself on the field — and even off the field — could be influential in pointing others to Jesus Christ.

As Case says, "You can choose to promote Christ, and that's been what I've strived to do ever since I stepped on the field."

Get ready now to "win the respect of outsiders."

On the Chalkboard

Don't leave your faith on the sidelines when you step onto the field.

A Case of Offense

Here are some of the statistics Case Keenum compiled while at Houston: He threw for more than five hundred yards in a single game. He threw for more than five thousand yards in one season. He also threw for at least three hundred yards in thirteen consecutive games.

Sports Stuff

The most common knee injury among football players is an injury to the anterior cruciate ligament (ACL). It is one of four major ligaments of the knee. The ACL extends from the femur (your thigh bone) to the tibia (your shin bone). When it is damaged, doctors repair it with a tendon from some other place in the body or from a donor.

Instant Replay

Which verse do I use to guide me when I compete? Who are some athletes I watch who are teaching me how to compete as a Christian?

The prayer of a righteous person
is powerful and effective.

James 5:16

PLAY BOOK ASSIGNMENT:
READ PSALM 138:1—3

You Figure It Out

Here's a mystery. Read it and try to figure out what happens.

A college basketball coach by the name of Jane Albright was attending her team's spring banquet. It was at the University of Wisconsin, where Jane was the women's coach, and her players were there to receive their awards for another successful season.

Jane was waiting for her turn to speak when she began to have a really, really bad headache. Not just one of those headaches that a little nap and a couple of Tylenol fixes. This was a major humdinger of a headache.

It got so bad that Jane had to be rushed to the hospital. As she lay on the hospital bed, she began to hear people talking about doing brain surgery.

On her!

The doctors had discovered that she was bleeding in her brain, and they were going to go in there and fix it.

When she heard that, Jane began to pray. At the same time, word was spreading to everyone who knew her or knew about her: "Jane is in bad shape. Pray for her."

As Jane lay there in that hospital room, she felt absolutely terrible. She began to realize that she might die. Instead of giving a speech at a basketball banquet, she could soon be having speeches made about her at her funeral. While doctors whispered all around her, she made a decision. In her pain, she prayed and told God that if he wanted to take her, he could take her. (Of course, he knew that already.) She was a Christian, and she told God she was ready to die.

A feeling of peace swept over her.

Soon the doctors took some more tests to make sure they knew what to fix when they opened up Jane's skull. To their surprise, their tests revealed that everything was ok.

The doctors were puzzled. All that blood from the bleeding—it was gone. They didn't know what had happened.

That's the mystery.

What happened to Jane? A bunch of well-trained, intelligent, hardworking doctors couldn't figure out what happened to her. Why did she get better without surgery? How did she remain alive?

You know the answer, don't you?

Jane does. "I really felt the power of prayer," she says as she recalls that surprising situation.

Prayer is the most amazing thing you'll ever see. Why not make it a habit to talk to God during the day?

It's not really a mystery, is it?

On the Chalkboard

If you're not talking with God, you don't have a prayer.

Women's Basketball

In the spring there is March Madness for both men's and women's NCAA basketball teams. But the women weren't in the NCAA until 1982. Before that, women college players were in the Association of Intercollegiate Athletics for Women (AIAW). In the first twenty-nine years of the NCAA women's tournament, the University of Tennessee won eight championships and the University of Connecticut won seven.

Sports Stuff

Girls basketball continues to grow. For girls who want to improve, the keys are: develop good ballhandling skills (dribbling and passing), be able to shoot (preferably a jump shot), and learn the ins and outs of the game by paying attention to the people who are really good. If you do those three things, and if you spend the needed hours practicing, you'll have a head start.

When was the last time I had a prayer answered? What was it? If it's been a while, should I be praying more?

A friend loves at all times, and a brother
is born for a time of adversity.

Proverbs 17:17

PLAY BOOK ASSIGNMENT:
READ ECCLESIASTES 4:9–12

Help from a Friend

Which team is the most famous in baseball? It's the one with the most World Series wins, the most history, the most tradition. The one on which the most famous baseball player ever played. The one with the most famous stadium—even though it's a replacement for the original.

Now imagine what it must be like to play for that team. To wear the famous pinstripes of the New York Yankees. The team of Babe Ruth, Lou Gehrig, Mickey Mantle, Derek Jeter, Mariano Rivera, and Joe DiMaggio.

Well, another guy named Joe once got traded to those same Yankees, and he was one unhappy guy. He didn't want to go.

He didn't want to live in New York, he didn't want to play in Yankee Stadium, and he didn't want to leave the team that traded him.

Joe Girardi was a catcher who was traded from the Colorado Rockies to the Yankees. Here's what he said about it: "I was scared to death. I was angry. I didn't understand why God would take me to New York."

What does a guy do in a situation like that?

What would you do? What do you do when you have to do something you do not want to do?

Here's what Joe did: He depended on his best friend.

In his case, his best friend was (and still is) his wife, Kim.

"It was amazing what Kim did for me during my first year in New York," Joe says. "She let me know that God had me there for a reason."

Joe didn't believe her, but he listened to what she said.

Within a year, Joe Girardi was jumping all over the Yankee infield, celebrating a World Series win. And he couldn't have done it without his best friend, Kim.

And then look at what happened later. A few years after that, after retiring as a player, Joe was named the manager of the Yankees. He went from being afraid of going to New York as a player to leading the Yankees to their first World Series championship in the twenty-first century.

How are you are at listening to good advice from friends?

Let's say a friend tries to encourage you. Do you shut him or her off? Or if a friend tries to give you some advice, do you say, "You're not my mother"?

Not a good idea.

Life is tough if we try to make it alone. That's why God put you in a family (yes, it's ok to take help from the people you eat breakfast with), and gave you friends. Notice that today's Game Plan verse mentions both friends and siblings.

"Two are better than one" (Ecclesiastes 4:9). Like Joe, be willing to listen to a friend who really cares.

On the Chalkboard

The first step in looking for help is to look for a friend.

Sports History Note

Joe Girardi played on the New York Yankees team that won three of the last four World Series played in the twentieth century. Then, in 2009, he was the manager when the Yankees won their next World Series—the twenty-sixth title in their franchise history.

Sports Stuff

Joe Girardi was especially valuable to his team as a player because he was a true leader. As a catcher, he knew how to help his pitchers get better. One of the things he was good at was knowing what the scouting report said (the team had a record of how other batters hit, which pitch they had trouble with, and things like that). Whichever sport you play, those are

158

two great characteristics: Make your teammates better by encouraging them and helping them, and study your opponents' strengths and weaknesses.

Instant Replay

Do I have one friend I can count on? Does this friend get me closer to God or farther from him?

We have different gifts, according to the
grace given to each of us.

Romans 12:6

PLAY BOOK ASSIGNMENT:
READ ROMANS 12:3–8

Music or Sports?

Sometimes, it's hard to decide which you are going to do: music or
sports.

Let's say you really like to play the piano, and you're starting
to get pretty good. But you also love soccer, and when you are
out there playing—well, there's nothing like it.

What are you going to do?

Do you have to pick one or the other? Is it important to
make a decision at your age? Can you tell which one God really
wants you to do?

Well, sometimes God lets people do both.

One person who started out pursuing sports and ended up pursuing music is Jonny Diaz. In 2010 he had his first hit song, "More Beautiful You." It's a great song that reminds teen girls that real beauty is not what they read about in fashion magazines.

Just a few years before Jonny's hit song, he enrolled at Florida State University to play baseball—just like his brother, Matt, who ended up playing major league baseball for several years.

But while at FSU, Jonny felt God's call on his life to concentrate on music. He gave up his baseball dreams to encourage people with godly music.

Another dual-love example is Ben Utecht. He graduated from the University of Minnesota and ended up playing football for the Indianapolis Colts. He has a Super Bowl ring to prove it. He was a member of the Colts in 2007 when they won the Vince Lombardi Trophy as Super Bowl champs.

But he soon began connecting with Christian musicians such as Jeremy Camp. Before he was done playing football, he had released his first album of Christian music. When Ben Utecht retired from football, he turned to a full-time music ministry.

Music or sports? You might be torn between the two—not knowing which God has in mind for you. At your age, stick with both. Keep practicing your flute or piano or trumpet. Keep singing. And keep kicking that soccer ball around.

God will show you the way he wants you to go—when it's time. He has gifted you purposefully so you can be used for his glory. He will show you the way.

> **On the Chalkboard**
>
> Sports and music are two languages that people in our world understand. It's ok to speak both.

More about Jonny and Ben

Both of these former athletes have websites where you can find out more about their God-honoring music and beliefs. If you don't get a chance to check out their websites, here are some interesting notes about Jonny and Ben. Jonny's mom is a writer who has penned several books and a number of magazine articles. His dad has been a spring-training chaplain for the Detroit Tigers. Ben's wife was a golfer at the University of Minnesota, and she was also crowned Miss Minnesota when she was a college student.

Sports Stuff

Some teens are able to keep being involved in both sports and music even into high school. This is something you need to be willing to discuss with your parents. They might be able to guide you toward the one they feel you can best use for God's glory. Also, this is where a youth pastor might be able to advise you later. For now, do your best and follow your heart.

Instant Replay

Right now which am I better at: music or sports? Should I set some goals for ways God can use my life in whichever of the two I am still involved with when I'm in high school?

I know what it is to be in need,
and I know what it is to have plenty.

Philippians 4:12

PLAY BOOK ASSIGNMENT:
READ PHILIPPIANS 4:10–13

Want Some Money?

How much is a lot of money to you?

Suppose your mom says, "Here's ten dollars. Go to the store and get a loaf of bread. You can keep the change." The eight dollars or so you get back in change would be a lot of money.

Or your dad says, "Here's ten dollars. Go to the bike shop and buy yourself a new twenty-one-speed bike." Yikes! Then the ten bucks would be a dinky amount of cash.

If your parents showed you how much money they get paid for their jobs, you'd probably think that would be a lot of money. But then if you compared their salary to say, an NBA basketball player, you'd stop wondering why your parents claim poverty once in a while. Many NBA players make as much as $20 million a year. Your parents would probably have to work for a couple of hundred years to earn that kind of money.

The point is, money is kind of a hard thing to figure out. It's hard to say what is a lot of it. Instead of worrying about that, the important thing for you right now is that you begin to develop godly ways to think about money.

Minor league baseball manager Brian Harper, who made a lot of money as a major leaguer after spending quite a few years squeaking by on nearly nothing as a minor leaguer, has some pretty good advice about money.

"The Bible says to be satisfied with what you have," says Harper, whose San Jose Giants won the California League championship in 2010. "I have been without, kind of like Paul said, and I have been with. I've been poor and I've been rich. The key is this: 'I can do all things through Christ who gives me strength.' The key is to put your trust in God."

Harper continues. "There's a verse in 1 Timothy 6 that I go by. It goes something like this: 'Command those who are rich in this world not to be arrogant or to put their trust in money, but to trust God who gives you those things to enjoy and to be generous in giving to others.'"

From what the Bible says about money, we can find at least three important rules to live by.

1. Our strength for everything, including thinking about money, comes from God.
2. If we have money, we shouldn't brag about it.
3. We should be generous with our money.

Whether you get a weekly $5 allowance or your parents are gazillionaires, those rules still apply. Think about that the next time you start thinking about money. And start now to develop a godly attitude about whatever money God allows you to have.

> **On the Chalkboard**
>
> **Count your blessings and count your money. But count on God, don't count on money.**

Money and Baseball

In one recent year, there were 433 players in the major leagues who earned a million dollars or more to play the game. Now, that's a lot of money! The highest paid player that year made $33 million. That's $203,703 a game!

Sports Stuff

You might think it's impossible that you would ever make money as an athlete. After all, you'll never be as good as Shaun White in snowboarding or Mark Sanchez in football or Ryan Howard in baseball. But there are thousands and thousands of young people each year who earn college scholarships because of their sports skills. Maybe that could be a long-range goal for you—to someday be a college athlete. Talk it over with your parents and ask them if your family wants to be committed to giving you the opportunities you need. Are there some youth sports organizations like AAU that you should get involved in as you try to reach your goal? Are there camps you should attend? Dream big.

Do I think I'd be happier if my parents made more money? What things do I think I need? What can God give me that money can't?

Those who are far from you will perish; ...
But as for me, it is good to be near God.
Psalm 73:27–28

PLAY BOOK ASSIGNMENT:
READ PSALM 73:1–17

What Happens When You're Good?

Have you been pretty good recently?

Cleaned your room when you were asked?

Didn't watch that bad movie some of your friends wanted to see?

Went to church without even complaining?

Fed the dog?

Even had devotions?

Now, that's being good.

So what happened? Did being good mean you got all A's in school? Did it mean you didn't make any mistakes in your soccer game? Did it mean your parents won the Publishers Clearing House grand prize? Did it mean your dad drove home a new Mustang convertible and said, "Hey, when you turn sixteen, it's yours"?

No, no, no, and no, right?

Life doesn't work that way, does it? Even if you are a Christian—and a pretty good one at that—God doesn't always give you immediate rewards for being good. Sure, he knows what you have done, and he promises to bless you for doing what he says, but he never said you would avoid all problems if you do the right thing.

Major league baseball shortstop Adam Everett knows that's true. Everett, who is an athlete proud to discuss his faith in Jesus Christ, played for the Detroit Tigers in 2010. He played hard and made only one error in the field through about half of the season.

As an older player (he was thirty-three), he also helped teach a younger shortstop the ropes of being a Tigers infielder. Everett did everything he could to help the team.

But in early July, the team let him go. Suddenly, no matter how good he was as a person, he was an unemployed baseball player. How could this happen?

A guy who probably wasn't a very good shortstop once wondered about the same kind of thing. The guy's name was Asaph, and we don't know what he was good at other than being a song leader for one of David's choirs.

Anyway, Asaph looked around like Adam Everett probably did and wondered why other people—especially ungodly people—were doing well while he—a godly guy—wasn't.

Here's what Asaph said: "You hold me by my right hand. You guide me with your counsel, and afterward you will take me into glory" (Psalm 73:23–24).

Asaph discovered that if he depended on God, God would always take care of him, no matter how bad things looked.

Forget Adam and Asaph for a minute. Think about yourself. Are you willing to trust God all the time—even when you seem to be having a grotesquely awful day?

When you're good and things go bad?

If you are willing to do that, then you know for sure that you really, truly trust God.

On the Chalkboard

Trusting God doesn't make your life perfect, but it does put your life into the hands of Someone who is.

Adam's Career

Never noted for being an exceptional hitter, Adam Everett used his glove to develop a respectable major league baseball career as a shortstop. Among his highlights: He was on the 2000 US Olympic team that won a gold medal; in 2006, he was named the top field shortstop in the majors; he finished second in balloting for National League shortstops for the 2004 All-Star Game.

174

Sports Stuff

When Adam Everett was growing up in Georgia, he was friends with Chad Sutter, whose dad, Bruce, was a Hall of Fame major league pitcher. He taught Adam a lot about baseball including three rules he thinks helped him make it himself: "Respect the game, run it out, and 'Don't make me boo you.'"

Instant Replay

Do I think God owes me anything because I am good? Or am I good because God deserves that from me?

Therefore, as we have opportunity, let us do good to all people, especially to those who belong to the family of believers.

Galatians 6:10

PLAY BOOK ASSIGNMENT: READ GALATIANS 6:7–10

Little Ant, Big Faith

If you like to watch great finishes in exciting basketball games, you need to see the YouTube clip of a national championship game from 2007.

In the NCAA Division II title contest, a little guy from tiny Barton College in Wilson, North Carolina, stole the show. And he stole the game from the opponents from Winona State.

With just forty-five seconds left in the game, Winona State led 73–67 and had a player at the free throw line. Everybody in the arena thought the game was over. You just don't come back from that far down that fast.

Well, everybody thought it was over but Anthony Atkinson—also known as, Lil Ant.

The 5' 9" guard from hometown Wilson was praying—asking for God's presence in this tough situation.

What happened over the next forty-five seconds was surreal. Here's a recap:

The Winona State player makes his free throw, so now it's 74–67.

Atkinson gets the ball, drives down the lane and scores. 74–69.

Barton fouls a Winona State player with thirty-five seconds left. He misses.

Atkinson gets himself open for a short jumper, which he makes. Now it's 74–71 with twenty-five seconds left.

Barton steals the inbound pass. The ball goes to Atkinson, who scores and is fouled: 74–73.

Lil Ant misses the free throw, but Barton fouls again to stop the clock with nineteen seconds left.

The Winona player misses the first shot and makes the second. Winona leads 75–73.

Atkinson drives from the left side and hits a reverse layup. It's 75–75 with seven seconds left.

As Winona brings the ball up court, a Barton player taps the ball for a steal. Atkinson picks it up and drives in for the game-winning layup as the buzzer goes off.

Barton 77, Winona State 75. Anthony Atkinson scored Barton's last ten points to win the game.

This mad finish by Lil Ant was nominated for an ESPY Award. Not long after this spellbinding finish, Anthony Atkinson signed up to play for the Harlem Globetrotters.

So, what is his goal as a professional athlete? Why did God answer his prayer back then? Atkinson says that it is for others. "If I can touch one person's life through my basketball, the deed is done." And he has proved that by sponsoring basketball teams and paying the fees for kids who can't afford it.

Anthony is an example of what we all should be. As believers in Jesus, we are here to help others—to "touch one person's life," as Lil Ant says.

As you think about the things you do and the things you are good at, can you find a way to use what God has given you to help other people? Start with your family. Do something for your family members, and then branch out to help others.

On the Chalkboard

Some people will never look for God if they don't see him in you.

The Globetrotters

The Harlem Globetrotters have been around since the 1920s. They have played more than 25,000 games all over the world. They combine comedy and basketball, and the players are known for their fancy ballhandling abilities. Check them out at *www.harlemglobetrotters.com*.

Sports Stuff

The cool thing about basketball is that you can practice your skills without anyone else around. All you need is a basketball and a flat surface. Here are some things you can teach yourself.

- Spinning the ball on your finger—It adds confidence and dexterity to your game.
- Spider drill—Stand up, crouch over, and dribble the ball in one spot on the floor between your feet. Alternate hands dribbling. Right. Left. Right behind your back. Left behind your back. Begin again. The ball always bounces on the same spot.
- Around the world—Simply practice moving the ball around your waste in a circle. Right hand to left hand and continue.
- Dribble figure eight—Start on your strong hand. Dribble to your side, then from the back push the ball between your feet. Continue the dribble with your off hand and go between your feet again, pushing it to your strong hand. Continue.

Instant Replay

Who do I know who needs me to be kind or helpful to him or her? What is one thing I can do at school or for my team that shows Jesus' love?

I call on the LORD in my distress,
and he answers me.

Psalm 120:1

PLAY BOOK ASSIGNMENT: READ 1 PETER 1:6–7

Don't Hit the Ref!

Rule number one in dealing with sport referees: Don't hit them.

That's pretty easy. Simply don't hit the ref.

But that's what Tara Snyder did. She didn't mean to. She's not a hothead. She's not a troublemaker.

Yet, bam!

Here's what happened. Tara was playing tennis in a tournament in England. She won the first set 7–6 and lost the second one 4–6. In the third set, she was behind 0–1 (if she loses the third set, she's out). Then it started raining. Tara asked for the officials to stop the match, but they didn't, and she lost the second game. So, now she's down 0–2.

That's when the umpire decided to stop play.

Tara was upset because she was down 0–2, making it really hard to come back. She turned to throw her racquet toward her bag, which was on the sidelines. She figured they were done playing, so what would it hurt?

Well, it hurt the sideline official it hit. Because her hand was wet, the racquet slipped when she threw it, and it nailed the guy in the shoulder. It didn't do any damage, really—just a glancing blow.

But Tara was in deep trouble now. The tournament officials decided to disqualify her from the tournament, and her name was blasted all over newspapers with the headline, "Snyder Hits Official!"

Embarrassed, Snyder sought assistance. "I really needed God's help to get through it. I prayed and asked him to show me what to do."

She felt that he wanted her to keep going and play in the next tournament, despite feeling that she would rather go home and forget about it.

"I've always believed that things happen for a reason and that God works everything out. When we're knocked down," she says, "he can give us strength to get right back up. He's made me stronger through the whole ordeal."

Have you done something recently that you wish you hadn't? Feeling embarrassed about it? Maybe a bit down? Do what Tara did. Turn it over to God. Pray to him honestly and tell him how you feel. Trust him that he really can take care of you even when you blow it. Then watch as he gives you the strength to get back up and going again.

There is nothing better you can do when you face trouble than to call on God. He'll forgive you and comfort you.

> **On the Chalkboard**
>
> **Give your troubles to God and turn trials into triumphs.**

Where Did We Get Tennis?

Most people who study tennis think it came from an eleventh-century game played in France. However, the game was not well known until the 1800s when courts began to be constructed in England. The first tennis club began in England in 1872.

Sports Stuff

Tennis is a sport in which good conduct is expected. There are several ways this can happen. First, as you warm up before a match, you try to hit the ball so that the other person can return it. This is not the time to hit winners or make your opponent run. Second, you should be fair in calling balls in or out, since it is your responsibility to do so when the ball is on your side of the net. Third, you should never distract another player while the ball is in play. This includes yelling, applauding, or in any other way being disruptive. Tennis is a sport where the Golden Rule applies (Matthew 7:12).

Instant Replay

What trouble have I gotten myself into? Have I been willing to talk it over with God?

Many are the plans in a person's heart,
but it is the LORD's purpose that prevails.

Proverbs 19:21

PLAY BOOK ASSIGNMENT:
READ 2 CORINTHIANS 1:15–17

Daily Checklist

Lots of people in sports keep a daily checklist.

Watch your coach next time you have practice. He or she will probably have a sheet of paper with a list of tasks to be accomplished at practice. Coach will mentally check them off as practice progresses.

Athletes often have a mental list of things they do before a game. From the time they leave home until the time they step onto the playing surface, they have things mapped out.

Sometimes athletes have some rather odd things on their daily checklist. Take a couple of NBA players, for instance. Caron Butler chewed on drinking straws during his games.

LeBron James's checklist always included grabbing a container of powder, putting some in his hands, and flinging them into the air as the powder creates a small cloud.

Checklists can be very helpful in your spiritual life too. Perhaps it would be a good idea to have a mental list of what you want to make sure happens each day as you try to live for God. To help you, here are four things professional tennis player Tara Snyder says helped her each day.

1. Stay focused. Don't get sidetracked, but keep your mind on what is important.
2. Surround yourself with positive spiritual people.
3. Ask God. Talk to God throughout the day, and he will give you guidance.
4. Put God first. Put him before sports, before everything.

In Proverbs we can see that God is in ultimate control, even when we set up our plans. No matter what our plans might be, if they are not plans that God would approve, they will not succeed.

Notice also that Paul made plans before he decided about his visits to Macedonia. He thought ahead of time about what he was going to do.

Why not try creating your own checklist? What four essential things do you think you need to do each day to build up your relationship with God and be the kind of person he wants you to be?

Then pray for God to guide you in what he wants you to do each day.

On the Chalkboard

No plan is a success unless God gives it his approval.

Speaking of Unique Checklist Items

Other odd things that athletes have had on their daily lists:

Hall of Fame baseball player Wade Boggs had to eat chicken before every game.

Hall of Fame NHL goaltender Patrick Roy talked to the goalposts during the game.

NBA player Mike Bibby clipped his fingernails during every game (and LeBron James always bit his).

Major league pitcher Turk Wendell brushed his teeth between each inning.

Tennis player Goran Ivanisevic always asked for the same ball he just hit if he hit an ace.

Sports Stuff

Make a list of goals for the sport in which you most want to show improvement. Find one thing for each of these areas:

1. improving my skills
2. improving my knowledge
3. improving my conditioning
4. improving my leadership

Instant Replay

If I do make plans, how do I know they are the things God wants me to do?

But when God ... called me by his grace ...

I went into Arabia.

Galatians 1:15, 17

PLAY BOOK ASSIGNMENT:
READ ACTS 9:1; 10:17—19

Late Bloomers

It's not easy being a late bloomer.

I ought to know. I was one.

Although I'm six feet tall now, I was "the short kid" for a long, long time while growing up.

It was a real problem when I turned thirteen and had to switch from the Little League field—where I was crushing Little League pitching—to the major league size field. Batting champ at age twelve. (Really! Wanna see the trophy?) Batting chump at age thirteen.

When baseball turned on me, I switched to loving basketball more than anything. But that just caused more problems. I had

"No. That'll slow me down," the son replied. "I'll be ok."

So, the high schooler braved the cold in order to improve his time. And by the time he was finished, he wasn't cold anyway. He crossed the finish line faster than he would have if he had been slowed down by too much clothing.

Whether you run on a cross-country team or not, you are in a race. And the best way to run that race is by taking off everything that might slow you down.

That's what the person who wrote the book of Hebrews said. He told us to toss off anything that slows us in our race for the Lord. For instance, if you have been doing something recently that you know is keeping you from God, throw it away. Or if there's something like music or spending too much time on the Internet that is keeping you from reading the Bible, throw it away (well, not literally—but put it aside).

What is the goal of a Christian? To be as close to God as possible. To reach that goal, sometimes we have to be a little uncomfortable.

The cross-country runner was pretty cold when he started the race, but he was rewarded by running better and even by not being too hot as he ran. By chucking his shirt, he ran better.

You will run your Christian race better if you don't have too much stuff slowing you down.

On the Chalkboard

You can't run God's race well if you have a backpack of extra stuff to carry around.

Speaking of Running

The North American record for marathons run in a lifetime is 965 by Norm Frank of Rochester, New York. He ran his first at age thirty-five in 1967. At age seventy-nine, health problems halted his dream of reaching 1,000 marathons. The world record is held by Horst Preisler of Germany. By the end of 2010, he had completed 1,670 marathons.

Sports Stuff

If you want to be a good long-distance runner, you need to build up a base of miles run. Each week, you need to set a goal of miles you want to run, then plan your week accordingly. The most important piece of equipment is the pair of shoes you wear. Make sure you get shoes designed for running (not basketball shoes) and have them fitted by a professional.

Instant Replay

What's slowing me down? How do I get rid of it?

I have become all things to all people so that
by all possible means I might save some.

1 Corinthians 9:22

PLAY BOOK ASSIGNMENT:
READ 1 CORINTHIANS 9:19–23

Hoops Roots

Do you know a lot about basketball—players' names, teams, stats, even some strategy?

That's good. But do you know anything about the game's history? Yes, history.

Before you stop reading because this isn't history class, let me tell you something about basketball that might really surprise you.

The sport was invented as a way to get the gospel of Jesus Christ to new people.

Yes, according to sports historian Dr. Tony Ladd of Wheaton College in Illinois, the inventor of basketball, Dr. James

Naismith, wanted the game to be used in missions work. Read what Dr. Ladd said of Naismith: "Perhaps he could reach people with a new game. As a committed Christian, he wanted to invent a game that would provide a means for him and others to lead other young men to a personal relationship with Christ." That game was basketball.

Imagine that!

And consider these: The NBA. Kevin Durant's skills. Your high school's team. Your basket in the driveway. These all exist because one man was looking for a way to spread the gospel.

Of course, it didn't turn out exactly as Dr. Naismith had planned, but there are still plenty of people who used basketball as a way to reach people and tell them about Jesus.

But there's something else we can learn. This can help us see that everything can be used for God.

If a sport like basketball can be invented as a way to help people know about God, then think about how some other things you have or do can be used that way. Paul set the example when he talked about doing whatever it takes to reach people for Jesus.

For instance, think about how your paper route can be a way to show God to people. By practicing honesty and reliability, you'll be a testimony.

Or what about your ability to play a musical instrument? That trumpet or drum can be dedicated to God.

Or your interest in animals. Could you find a way to use that as an encouragement to others who like them too?

If basketball can be used for Jesus, there shouldn't be anything stopping us from using our interests for him.

Basketball Begins

The first basketball game was played in late 1891. In the early days of the game, there were nine players on a team. A player could not run with the ball; he had to throw it after catching it. If a team made three straight fouls, the other team got a point. A goal was scored when someone would either throw or bat the ball into the goal. If the ball went out of bounds, it belonged to the first person touching it. Somehow, this game caught on. In December 2010, the original thirteen rules for basketball, penned by James Naismith 119 years earlier, were sold at auction for $4.3 million.

Sports Stuff

If you are really into sports but you know that you won't ever be the next John Wall or Sidney Crosby, you might want to consider an alternate career in sports. Maybe you'll want to someday study sports management and work on the staff for a pro team. Or if you are a good writer, think about becoming a journalist who gets to cover the games and interview the athletes. Even computer guys are needed by pro teams to run their websites and such. Think of ways you might stay in sports even though you might not ever wear a college or pro uniform.

Instant Replay

What can I use for God that I have never thought of using before?

As for those who were held in high esteem—
whatever they were makes no difference to
me; God does not show favoritism.

Galatians 2:6

PLAY BOOK ASSIGNMENT: READ 1 TIMOTHY 2:1–6

The $275,000,000 Man

In 2008, the New York Yankees signed Alex Rodriguez to a contract that promised to pay him $275 million.

Do you know how much that is? For one thing, if the Rodriguez family were to spend a thousand dollars a day, they would not run out of money until the year 2761 (753 years). You could buy 3,235 Corvettes, loaded. If you gave 10 percent to your church, the board would have more than $27 million with which to do some good things (maybe they'd build a gym).

But did you know that Alex Rodriguez, who didn't win a championship until 2009—fifteen years into his career—*is not worth any more than you are?* Even with his $275 million, you and A-Rod have the exact same value.

The value of a person is not found in how much money he has but in how much God cherishes that person. And when you think about it, you'll realize that you and Alex share this: You are both so valuable to God that he was willing to sacrifice his only Son, Jesus, for you.

Rich people, poor people, and everyone between the two. None of that makes a person more valuable than another. Jesus Christ "gave himself as a ransom [a payment] for all people" (1 Timothy 2:6). He died for all people the same.

So, what does that mean to you?

Do you ever have times when you are sitting in your bedroom wondering about life? Do you ever think that you make too many mistakes to be worth much to anybody? Or that you can't really do all the neat stuff your older brother does? Or that everybody seems to be on your case all the time? Or that you're too ugly or have teeth that are too big or have really bad hair?

When you begin to feel that way, it's easy to think you're not worth much. But remember this: When Jesus died on the cross, he was saying that you were worth dying for. Jesus would have died for you if you were the only person on earth.

God was willing to exchange his Son for you. Whoa! That shows how much value he places on you.

So whether you make $275 million playing baseball or $8.98 a week on a paper route, you are special to God. Don't let anyone tell you differently.

Speaking of Money

A bunch of other baseball players have also landed contracts for more than $150 million. A few names in this tier include: Derek Jeter, $189 million; Joe Mauer, $184 million; Mark Teixeira, $180 million; CC Sabathia, $161 million; Manny Ramirez, $160 million; Troy Tulowitzki, $157 million; and Miguel Cabrera, $152 million.

Sports Stuff

Who is my favorite sports figure? Does how much he makes help me decide whether I value him or not? What makes an athlete important to me? Have I ever thought about setting up some guidelines for the kind of person I want to follow?

◄ Instant Replay

What makes me sometimes think I'm not worth much? How does thinking about God's sacrifice help me not to get down on myself?

Whoever dwells in the shelter of the Most
High will rest in the shadow of the Almighty.
Psalm 91:1

**PLAY BOOK ASSIGNMENT:
READ PSALM 91**

The Levite and the QB

There's not a lot of similarity between a guy playing quarterback in the NFL and a Levite serving in an Old Testament temple. One calls the signals in front of tens of thousands. The other wrote a testimony of God's trustworthiness.

And one NFL signal-caller really, really likes the words written by one Levite.

In an article in *Sports Spectrum* magazine, quarterback Aaron Rodgers reveals his thoughts on Psalm 91: "The Lord gave me that passage my junior year of high school ... every time I get injured, or am scared, or have a bad day, I go back to that passage."

Did you read it? Psalm 91, that is.

You can see why Aaron would like it. As a quarterback, he faces a lot of pressure. The success of an entire team—and even the joy of thousands of people in an entire city—rests on how well he plays the game of football.

So what is so special about Psalm 91?

Verse 1: We can rest securely in God's shadow. No matter what kinds of bad things happen, God overshadows us with his love.

Verse 2: God is our refuge. Do you ever have a hard time with something and you can't wait to get back to your own bedroom? You close the door, and you feel safe and secure. God is like that for us. Also, God is our fortress. That's like having a great snow wall to hide behind when you're in a big snowball fight.

Verse 3: When stuff happens, and you feel trapped (you have to write a report on your state capital tomorrow, and you can't think of a word to write), God will provide a covering for you. (You still have to write the paper, but you can talk to God about it for help and comfort.)

With a little help from your mom or dad, or from another adult who really knows the Bible, you could go through each verse of Psalm 91 and find help.

A lot of people have said a lot of good things about Aaron Rodgers, the quarterback. But maybe the best thing you can say about him is that he taught you to trust God in a new way by introducing you to Psalm 91.

Life has a way of scaring all of us. But like Rodgers, be ready to trust God whenever you are frightened.

> ## On the Chalkboard
>
> **When you are struggling with fear and doubt, use Psalm 91 to figure things out.**

Speaking of Quarterbacks

Do you know who Aaron Rodgers replaced when he became a first-string NFL quarterback? Here's a hint: Green Bay. Yes, Rodgers replaced Brett Favre, who had been the Packers' starting quarterback for sixteen straight years. When it was time for Rodgers to become the Packers' top quarterback after Favre left the team, Aaron had only played in a grand total of seven games.

Sports Stuff

Want to play quarterback? Here are some tips for young quarterbacks from an NFL star

1. Work on your footwork. Jumping rope is good for that.
2. Learn to recognize what the defense is doing. Especially pay attention to the safeties.
3. Don't compare yourself with others. Others will be faster, stronger, and so forth. Just be the best YOU can be.

Instant Replay

What things in life frighten me the most? What have I already discovered in Psalm 91 that can help me?

Whoever gives heed to instruction prospers.

Proverbs 16:20

PLAY BOOK ASSIGNMENT: READ EPHESIANS 6:1–3

Why Bother with School?

How's school?

That's one subject everyone has an opinion about.

Some kids love it. Some, well, don't love it. Some just shrug their shoulders and say, "It's ok, I guess."

Even if you love school, it is sometimes hard to come up with a really good reason why you have to spend all those long hours in class.

Think about it. What difference does it make that you can name all the states and capitals? Will you ever have to multiply mixed fractions in real life? Someday when you're a computer technician, will it matter that a cell has a nucleus? Or when you're in the middle of raising your kids in the far distant future, will it really matter that the tallest mountain in North America is Mt. McKinley? And reelee, dus it reeelly madder if yu ken spel gud?

Of course, if you're planning a career being a contestant on *Jeopardy*, these things might come in handy. And that kind of knowledge sure helped the people on *Are You Smarter Than a Fifth Grader*. But come on, is that any reason to study every night and do all that homework? Does a report on Peru make you a better person?

In other words, why study? Why mess with all that school stuff? Is God involved in that at all?

Perhaps. Let's look at two reasons why you might think so.

First, doing well in school is a good way to obey God when he talks about how to treat your parents. You know the verses in the Bible that say, "Honor your father and mother." Did you know that you honor them when you succeed in school?

Listen to A.C. Green, longtime NBA star. He says he didn't care much for good grades at first, but then something changed. He decided he should get good grades so he could honor his parents. "By the time I got to my junior year, my greatest goal was to be on the honor roll. I wanted my name on our school board that was right by the front door. I wanted to bring my parents in to see my name on that board. That made me work harder." It may seem weird to you now, but your success is a way of showing your parents how important they are to you. They want you to succeed, and when you do, they feel great.

A second reason to study is that God expects your best at all times. "Whatever you do, work at it with all your heart, as working for the Lord, not for human masters" (Colossians 3:23). If you play sports, you usually don't need this reminder. You're having so much fun running around out there it's easy to do that with all your might. It comes naturally because you're having a great time.

But schoolwork is another ball game completely. With school, you might need to remind yourself who you are doing this for. The best way to make sure you get the most out of the brain God gave you is to do your work for him, not for others.

There are two good reasons to hit the books: to honor your parents and to work for God.

Now, who was the thirty-seventh president of the United States?

On the Chalkboard

One good thing about an education is that it helps you realize you don't know everything.

A.C. Green's Principles

In A.C. Green's book, *Victory*, he spells out fifty-two principles for living a godly life. One of those principles regarding learning states, "Admit you don't know everything. Open yourself up to learn from others. Develop a teachable spirit." You can research A.C. Green to learn more about the man, his foundation, and his goals for making our communities a better place for all.

Sports Stuff

More than a few students have missed out on playing varsity sports because they didn't have good grades. If you want to make sure you are ready to get the grades you need when you are in high school sports, you need to start now to develop good study habits. Do you keep an assignment book? Do you make sure each assignment is complete each day? Do you know how to study for tests? These things will help you in school and in sports.

Instant Replay

What do I think of school? Have I ever thought about how my attitude toward learning and school reflects on my relationship with God?

That is why, for Christ's sake, I delight in
weaknesses ... For when I am weak, then I
am strong.

2 Corinthians 12:10

**PLAY BOOK ASSIGNMENT:
READ 2 CORINTHIANS 4:16–18**

The Pain

What could be better than being a major league baseball player? When you go to work, you take a ball glove, not a lunch pail. Instead of slaving over a calculator figuring out a budget, you get to walk up to home plate with a baseball bat in your hand.

Your workday goes like this: Go to a baseball park, put on a major league uniform, take batting practice, take fielding practice, play a game, talk to some reporters, take a shower, and go home.

That's your job!!

And you get treated like a king for doing this.

Imagine, though, that your job is to be a professional athlete who has to be able to run fast, hit ninety-mph fastballs, and play first base—all while suffering from arthritis.

Usually, we think of arthritis as being something Grandma has. But you may be like Rico Brogna, who played first base in the major leagues with that disease. You may be young and have arthritis.

If you do, you know about the stiffness in your joints, about how hard it is to get out of bed in the morning, about how activity that is supposed to be fun for everyone else just makes the pain worse.

Rico Brogna, who was one of the best first basemen in the big leagues, played while suffering from ankylosis spondylitis (AS), a type of arthritis that affects the bones and joints. He describes how AS slowed him down before he discovered what it was: "I tried to play with pain in my hips and spine. I walked like I was crippled, and I couldn't even bend over to tie my shoes."

Once he was diagnosed, the pain didn't go away, but he found out that exercise and medication could help.

But Rico had another source that helped him. He was a strong Christian who knew that even the problems with AS can have positive results. "It's during difficult times," he said, "that God brings me closer to himself. What I first thought was devastation has turned into an unbelievable blessing."

Whether you have arthritis or some other physical problem—or even if you have totally different tough problems—you can learn a lot from this baseball player.

God doesn't allow illness and trouble into our lives without giving us the strength to handle them and the hope that he has something better for us later.

So, don't give up when you are down. Lean on Jesus, as Rico Brogna did when he was playing ball and as he still does as a minor league baseball coach, and see what God can teach you.

> ### On the Chalkboard
>
> **The real problem with pain comes when we let it hurt our relationship with God.**

Others Who Suffered

Several athletes have played at the highest levels despite serious illnesses and difficulties. Baseball pitcher Jon Lester came back from cancer surgery and treatment to star for the Boston Red Sox. Josh Hamilton, 2010 American League MVP, came back from a serious addiction to illegal drugs. The most famous is Lou Gehrig, a New York Yankee player of the 1920s and 1930s. He suffered from amyotrophic lateral sclerosis (ALS), which has become known as Lou Gehrig's disease.

Sports Stuff

One advantage athletes have today over athletes of twenty or thirty years ago is that there are many more doctors who specialize in sports medicine now. Someone like Rico Brogna was able to play because doctors and therapists knew how to treat him. If you have a sports-related injury, don't ignore it. If some part of your body is in pain for a long period of time (not just a sore muscle or a bruise), have someone check you over.

Instant Replay

What do I suffer from? How can I begin to trust God with my problem? How can it make me closer to God?

This is how God showed his love among us:
He sent his one and only Son into the world.

1 John 4:9

PLAY BOOK ASSIGNMENT:
READ 1 JOHN 4:7–10

The Last Ball of the Century

The last baseball player to record a putout in the twentieth century was Chad Curtis of the New York Yankees. While playing left field for the Yankees in the 1999 World Series, Curtis caught the final out of game four of the Series, which New York swept 4–0 over the Atlanta Braves.

When Curtis caught the last ball to end the game, the Series, and the century, Chad realized he had something very significant in his possession. So he squeezed the ball and made sure he took it with him. Even through the mad celebration that took place on the field, Chad hung on to that baseball. He intended to keep it for a souvenir.

That night, Chad climbed into his car and began the long drive to his home in Michigan. While driving through the night, Curtis thought about that ball lying next to him on the passenger seat of the car. He decided that instead of keeping it for himself, he would give it to a friend in New York who had helped the Curtis family during the season.

Chad thought of God, who had someone very special with him in heaven. That special person was Jesus. God wanted to keep Jesus with him, but he also knew that he could help us by giving Jesus to die for us. So, with pain in his heart, God gave us Jesus.

Chad thought about that ball and decided that if God could give us Jesus, he shouldn't have any trouble giving his friend that baseball. So that's what he did.

Did you ever have something you didn't want to give up? Something special and close to your heart? Remember what it took for you to give that up? Imagine how it hurt God to send Jesus from perfect heaven to dusty, old, sinful earth. And to watch him die so horribly.

For Chad and for us, giving up a baseball is a tiny picture of what God did for us in sending Jesus as our Savior.

On the Chalkboard

We can never give up anything that comes close to what God gave up for our salvation.

Chad the Hero

Only a very few times in major league history has anyone hit what is called a "walk-off" home run in the World Series. That means the home run is a late-inning winning run that wins the game and everyone walks off the field. Three famous ones are Bill Mazeroski's 1960 blast that beat the New York Yankees in game seven that year, Kirk Gibson's ninth-inning home run to beat the A's in game one of the 1988 Series, and Joe Carter's ninth-inning home run that propelled the Toronto Blue Jays to their 1993 win over the Philadelphia Phillies. In 1999, Chad Curtis hit one of those. Batting in the tenth inning of game three, Chad blasted a round-tripper that gave the Yankees a three-game lead over the Braves. The next day, New York completed the sweep of the Braves, four games to none.

Sports Stuff

Hitting a home run is not as easy as it looks. But you don't have to be as big as Ryan Howard to hit them. Chad is 5' 10" and weighs 185 pounds. And the greatest home run hitter in baseball history, Hank Aaron, was not a big person. The keys to Aaron's success (755 home runs) were quick hands, strong wrists, and great timing. Additional tips for good hitting include:

- Coordinate all parts of the swing together, making sure your swing results in one smooth motion.
- Get the fat part of the bat on the ball, which is about the middle of the barrel of the bat.

- Keep the head from pulling away, which means your face doesn't turn away from the action of the ball hitting the bat.
- Stride toward the pitcher's mound with your front foot, not away from it.

Have I ever thought of how God felt to see his Son crucified, knowing that his decision had sent him to earth?

You'll climb in the car with Mom, who will drive you thirty-five minutes to the wrong field. And you'll finally arrive at the correct field with two minutes to go in the third quarter.

You'll have your best week of practice ever and then hurt your ankle in warm-ups before the big game.

This kind of stuff happens all the time to kids who play sports. They get bum deals. And they have to learn to deal with it in an un-bum-like way.

Todd Walker was an infielder in the major leagues for several years. He was pretty good too. One year, he hit .316. But before he got that kind of success, he had his own series of bum deals.

One of the biggest bummers came when he began his rookie year in the major leagues. Walker had been an outstanding college player, and the year before he got to the major leagues, he was the Player of the Year in his level of the minor leagues. He was expected to become a big star.

But when he got to Minnesota to play for the Twins, he stopped hitting. Through the first two months of his first season, his batting average was only .194. If you don't know how bad that is, it means that he was getting a base hit less than two times for every ten times he batted.

That's when he got some really bad news. On his twenty-second birthday, he received a note from the Twins that said he was being sent back down to the minors.

Be honest. What would you do if you got such bad news? Pout? Hit something? Yell and scream? Cry? Send a really sad tweet to Mom? Blame somebody?

Here's what Todd did. He trusted God.

"Was I mad at God?" he says. "No, not really. Sure, God could have allowed me to stay in the big leagues. But I think I learned a lot more by being sent down. You learn the most from your biggest failures. I looked to God for strength. The Bible says to put all your worries on the Lord, and that's what I try to do."

Now, there's an idea. Turn everything over to Jesus. Try that the next time you get a bum deal.

On the Chalkboard

Why get mad at God when trusting him is the way to succeed?

Getting to Know Todd Walker

Todd Walker has to have a rather large trophy case. It would have to hold his trophy for being the Louisiana High School Baseball Player of the Year. There would have to be room for his All-State plaque for soccer when he was in high school. Over in the corner could be the three awards he received for being All-American in baseball all three years he went to Louisiana State University. Not to mention having room for his NCAA Freshman of the Year Award, his trophy for being the College World Series Player of the Year, and the award from *Baseball Digest* magazine, which named him the best collegiate second baseman for an entire decade. In 2009, he was named to the College Baseball Hall of Fame.

Sports Stuff

How you handle a tough spot in sports can make you or break you as an athlete. One of the best ways to practice making sure a disappointment on the court doesn't bother you is by not showing your emotions when a bad thing happens. When you play table tennis, for instance, practice staying the same whether you miss a shot or nail a winner. If you start training yourself not to get mad when you fail, you'll become a calmer player in all your sports.

Instant Replay

What bum deal have I received recently? How can I turn that into something that helps me get closer to God, not farther from him?

We are therefore Christ's ambassadors.

2 Corinthians 5:20

PLAY BOOK ASSIGNMENT:
READ 2 CORINTHIANS 5:16-20

Giving Hope

It's time for a little lesson in Español—Spanish.

If you already know the answer to this, be patient. Maybe another time you'll get a question that's more challenging.

Ok, here goes. What is the Spanish word for "hope"?

Is that your final answer?

Before we get to the answer, you need to read about a person who has found a way to give hope to some people in a poor country. The guy's name is Dave Valle, and he was at one time a catcher in major league baseball. He caught for the Seattle Mariners for several years and ended his career while he was with the Texas Rangers. One year he was good enough to lead the American League in throwing out runners trying to steal.

Toward the end of his career, he and his wife, Vicky, decided that they wanted to do something to help people in the world who didn't have all the nice stuff they had. Quite a few years before, Dave had played some baseball in the Dominican Republic (you get ten extra points if you can point to it on a map). While there, he fell in love with the people, and he noticed that they didn't have much.

So, when Dave and Vicki thought of helping people, they decided to help Dominicans. And guess what they called their new ministry? They called it Esperanza, which means ... well, you know what it means.

Here's what the Valles did. They started a bank in the Dominican Republic that loans money to women. The women then can start their own small businesses with the money. In that way, the women have hope of earning a living. And, when the women get together at their "bank" meetings, someone tells them about Jesus Christ. By 2010, Esperanza had granted 75,000 loans worth almost $15 million.

Do you ever think much about missionary work, about the work Christians do to take hope to people in other countries? Have you ever thought about how you might have a small part in helping missionaries and their work?

Dave and Vicki Valle realized that they were "Christ's ambassadors," so they found a way to give hope. Is what they are doing limited to adults? How can you give hope?

Could you and your family sponsor a Bank of Hope through Esperanza? Check out *www.esperanza.org*.

Could you support a child through World Vision or some other organization? Research foundations and sites like *www.worldvision.org*.

Could you put together a shoebox package for Samaritan's Purse? Investigate information at *www.samaritanspurse.org*.

Could you email a missionary family from your church and see if there's anything you can do to help them?

Could you help serve Thanksgiving dinner with your parents at a mission in your city?

Could you offer hope, or *esperanza*? Of course you can. God gave you hope. Now share it.

> **On the Chalkboard**
>
> **When you have the hope of the world, you have a responsibility to a hopeless world.**

Dominican Baseball

The country that Dave and Vicki Valle help has been one of the top sources for major league baseball players. One particular city, San Pedro de Macoris, has sent more than seventy-five players to the big leagues—including one very well known second baseman named Robinson Cano.

Sports Stuff

Dave Valle would admit it. He wasn't a very good hitter. Three times when he was in the majors, his batting average was below what they call the Mendoza line: .200. So how did Valle stay in the majors for thirteen years? He was a specialist. Sometimes it pays to learn how to do one thing and do it very well. For Valle, one thing he did well was throw out runners. So, being a good defensive catcher helped him have a long career. What can you specialize in so your coaches will notice you and you can help the team? While working on all your skills, pick one thing and become an expert at it—soccer (dribbling), basketball (ball-handling), baseball (bunting), volleyball (setting), hockey (handling the stick).

Instant Replay

What is my impression of missionaries? Could I ever see God using me in this way? Are there any smaller things I should be doing now for missions?

Tie them as symbols on your hands
and bind them on your foreheads.

Deuteronomy 6:8

PLAY BOOK ASSIGNMENT:
READ DEUTERONOMY 6:1–9

Little Reminders

It's time for a really big word that might be able to help you in a little way.

Ready for the word? "Mnemonics."

The first letter is silent, and it is pronounced "ni-mon-iks."

And here's what it means: a short mental technique that helps you memorize or remember something.

If you play the piano, you might know this one: Every good boy does fine. That little sentence helps you recall that the treble clef notes are EGBDF.

Sometimes it is good for us to have these little devices handy when we are trying to remember important spiritual truths as well. A few years ago, one of the most popular mnemonic devices was a wristband that read: WWJD. It was designed to remind the wearer to ask: What Would Jesus Do? in every situation that might arise.

Another popular one is FROG: Fully Rely On God.

One football player who made good use of mnemonic devices was Julian Vandervelde, who played on the offensive line for the University of Iowa. He wrote two reminders on the tape that was wrapped around his right and left wrists during the games.

On the left wrist, Julian wrote 2 Timothy 1:7, which says, "For the Spirit God gave us does not make us timid, but gives us power, love and self-discipline." Then he wrote this mnemonic: AO1. What do you think that meant?

On his right wrist, Julian wrote Proverbs 21:31 for home games: "The horse is made ready for the day of battle, but victory rests with the Lord." For away games he wrote Psalm 3:6, which says, "I will not fear though tens of thousands assail me on every side." And at both home and away games he wrote the mnemonic G2G. Any ideas what that meant?

In the middle of a hard fought game, Vandervelde could always look down at his wrists and be reminded of his main goals as a football player: To remember that he played for an "Audience of One (AO1)" and to give the "Glory to God (G2G)."

What reminders do you need as you try to honor God with your life?

It's not an original idea with Julian. God told the Israelites to do something similar in Deuteronomy 6. He wanted them to be reminded how he had helped them in the past, so he told them to keep some reminders on their hands and on their foreheads.

Is there a set of letters that might help you be the kind of person you know God wants you to be.

BKTO? Be Kind to Others?

ADYB? Always Do Your Best?

WTGTP? When Things Get Tough, Pray?

Why not come up with your own reminders. Put them on your notebook or on the tip of your basketball shoes.

A little reminder might be a big help in your life.

> **On the Chalkboard**
>
> **God is unforgettable, but sometimes we forget how to honor him.**

Sports Stuff

If you want to have a little reminder with you if you are playing on a team sport, make sure it's not against the rules. Sometimes leagues don't allow you to have anything extra written on your shoes or tape. Even NFL players have gotten into trouble for messages on their hats or shoes, so check with a coach first.

Instant Replay

What do I think is the most important spiritual idea for me to remember? Would I be embarrassed to have some kind of reminder on my notebook or shoes?

But I trust in you, LORD; I say, "You are my God." My times are in your hands.

Psalm 31:14–15

PLAY BOOK ASSIGNMENT: READ PSALM 31:1–15

A Second Chance

Did you ever try something that didn't work out very well — and you wish you had a second chance to do it better?

Maybe it was the school spelling bee, and you knew how to spell "ramification," but you spelled it "ramafication." Nobody said, "Oh, that's not right. Give it another try."

Or perhaps you were in a school play and all you had to say on the big night was, "But Mr. Smith, nobody goes to that store anymore," and you said, "But Mr. Smith, nobody goes to that more any store."

All of us have times when we wish we had a second chance. Rebekah Bradford got a second chance. Twice, actually.

Rebekah is a speed skater—one of those sports that becomes really popular during the Winter Olympics because it is so fast and so exciting.

She was trying out for the US Olympic team that was going to compete in Vancouver in 2010. It was December 30, 2009, and it was the last chance she would have to make the US team. She began her 1,000-meter race, and everything was going well. But with just about twenty feet left before she got to the finish line, Rebekah fell. She failed to qualify.

Obviously, she was bummed to the max. Imagine working all your life for something—and you get within twenty feet of it only to lose it.

But then something really odd happened. She was told that she had another chance. The rule stated, apparently, that if she wanted to she could try again.

She did, and this time she didn't fall down. She qualified and was a member of the US Olympic team in 2010.

But you know what? This was not the first time she got a second chance. God gave her one too.

She grew up in a Christian home, but she didn't want to put her faith in Jesus Christ. She had turned skating into her religion. But while that may get someone to Vancouver, it sure can't get you to heaven.

So for a long time, she rejected Jesus.

However, a few years before she would appear in the Olympics, she went to church one more time. And she heard the gospel once again. God had given her a second chance to accept Jesus—and she did.

On that December day in 2009 when she failed and then got a second skating chance, she had begun the day with a verse

Do you know Jesus? Have you met him by putting your faith in his death on the cross for you? Have you asked him to be your Savior, which means you can then talk with him and develop a real relationship with him?

Please don't do like I did with Pete. Before I got a chance to meet him, it was too late. Make sure you get to know Jesus Christ before you don't have a chance to anymore.

Meet Jesus. Really get to know him.

On the Chalkboard

Knowing about Jesus is no substitute for knowing him.

More about Pete

Pete Maravich played ten years in the NBA. One year, he led the league in scoring with thirty points a game. But all the time he played, he knew he was missing something. When he was eighteen, he had rejected the opportunity to trust Jesus as his Savior. When he was in his mid-thirties, he finally realized how important it is to become a Christian. After getting saved, Pete was a great evangelist. He went around the country telling young basketball fans that despite having earned millions of dollars and becoming incredibly famous, the best thing that happened to him was becoming a Christian. He died on January 5, 1988, while playing pickup basketball with Dr. James Dobson, who was the founder of Focus on the Family.

Sports Stuff

Before Pete Maravich died, he produced a series of basketball videos called "Homework Basketball." One of the things he emphasized in those videos was the importance of doing drills. If you want to spend the time it takes to get better at your sport, you need to repeat certain skills over and over and over. With basketball, doing dribbling and ballhandling drills are essential. They help you handle the ball as second nature, not as something that is difficult. In baseball, you can break down fielding your position into sections and work on each part of fielding with drills (for instance, practice fielding ground balls and making the transfer of ball to glove to throwing position). You can always develop your own drills for the sport you play.

Instant Replay

Am I sure I know Jesus? Who can I talk with to help me if I have doubts?

The one who sows righteousness
reaps a sure reward.

Proverbs 11:18

Whoever sows injustice reaps calamity.

Proverbs 22:8

PLAY BOOK ASSIGNMENT:
READ GALATIANS 6:7—10

Throwing It All Away

This guy was good!

He could catch passes most people didn't even wave at. Opposing players looked like high school kids next to this college star.

This athlete was such a good receiver that most people were ready to give him the Heisman Trophy without even voting on it. There was no doubt he was the best player in the land. And the land had a bunch of good players.

But then our hero forgot something. He didn't forget to run the right routes for his quarterback. He didn't forget how to wrap his strong fingers around the pigskin.

He forgot one of God's laws.

You know this law. It's the one your parents might remind you about when you don't turn in your homework. Or when you try to sneak around and do something you aren't supposed to.

It's the law from God that says whatever you sow, that's what you'll reap. If you plant corn in your garden, don't expect to come back in two months and pick tomatoes. And if you plant sin, don't expect to turn around and find God blessing you.

The Heisman Trophy candidate forgot the law when he went into a store and walked out with hundreds of dollars of merchandise that he didn't completely pay for. Of course, he also forgot to check for a store security camera, which caught the deed on tape—but that's another story.

As a result of stealing these clothes, the football star was dropped from consideration for the Heisman Trophy. He sowed dishonesty and he reaped embarrassment. He gained some new clothes, but he lost some pretty impressive hardware.

God wasn't kidding. He meant it when he had Paul write this verse: "Do not be deceived: God cannot be mocked. A man reaps what he sows" (Galatians 6:7).

Do you know how much God cares for you? He cares enough to let you know how things work in his world. He doesn't make up stuff after we do it and say, "Ha! Ha! I caught you." No, he says, "Listen, my child. Let me give you some help. If you do bad things, other bad things will follow. But if you do good things, you will be honored." Sowing. Reaping. It's pretty clear.

The football player knew that. But he thought just this once he could sneak by without consequence. Bad idea for him. Bad idea for you.

God loves you, and he wants what's best. Listen to what he tells you.

On the Chalkboard

If you go looking for trouble, it will find you.

Heisman Talk

Here are some Christian Heisman Trophy winners and an interesting fact about each.

- Archie Griffin is the only player to ever win the Heisman Trophy twice. (Ohio State; 1974, 1975)
- Charlie Ward was never drafted by the NFL, so he went on to play in the NBA for the New York Knicks. (Florida State; 1993)
- Danny Wuerffel played for the New Orleans Saints. After his NFL career ended, he worked in a ministry in New Orleans. His home was destroyed in Hurricane Katrina in 2005. (Florida; 1996)
- Tim Tebow was homeschooled in high school. His parents are missionaries in the Philippines. (Florida; 2007)
- Sam Bradford was a leader in the Fellowship of Christian Athletes at his university. (Oklahoma; 2008)

Sports Stuff

Does it matter to your team what you do when you are not with them? Lots of athletes are finding out that it does. First, when you are not with the team it is a good time to work on things that will make you a better player. Second, many athletes make wrong decisions when they are out on their own. They might get hurt doing something foolish or they might get into trouble. In either case, these athletes let their teammates down because they can't participate as they should. So, remember that you are always a part of the team, even when the team is not with you.

◄ Instant Replay

Do I realize that my parents love me when they try to help me avoid trouble—even though I think they are too strict? Do I realize they are trying to do what God wants them to?

Pray continually.

1 Thessalonians 5:17

PLAY BOOK ASSIGNMENT: READ ROMANS 1:8–10

Smart as a Football Player

The quarterback drops back to pass. It's a blitz! He runs to his right. He looks up. He fires the ball downfield. His wide receiver has his man beat! He reaches up. He makes the catch! He's at the twenty. The ten. The five. Touchdown!!!!

You're watching the game on your TV at home, and you see the wide receiver do something the TV announcer doesn't mention. The player who just scored the touchdown crosses the goal line, stops, points up into the air, and then kneels on one knee and prays.

What's going on here?

This display of faith is not welcomed by everyone. Some people don't like football players to bring their faith onto the field by praising God and then praying after scoring a touchdown. And some people who appreciate prayer may even have a question about what such a prayer says. Does it suggest that God cares for one person over another?

No matter what other people think about this practice, it does mean one thing for sure. The athlete who scored the touchdown realizes that prayer can happen anywhere. And he may even be trying to live out this important biblical teaching: "Pray continually."

Ever wonder what in the world that verse in 1 Thessalonians means? Does it mean that we can do only one thing in life: pray? Does it mean we can't eat, sleep, wash the dishes (you wish), study (you double wish), or enjoy a good game of tiddlywinks? Are we supposed to be monks, sitting around all day chanting prayers?

To find out what it means, look at Romans 1:8–10. In those verses, Paul (a very active guy, who although he was not a football player was definitely not a monk) said that his continual prayer went like this: "Constantly I remember you in my prayers at all times" (vv. 9–10). It means that as he did other things, he kept prayer requests for his Roman friends in mind. Then he could pray for them regularly.

Think back over your day today or yesterday. How often did you pray? Was it continual? Was it regular?

For some football players, crossing the goal line has become a reminder to pray.

You can develop reminders. For instance, take a Post-it note packet and write some requests on the pages. Then stick them on your textbooks. When you open your book bag and find the note that says, "Mom's job problems," you'll remember to pray a quick prayer for your mom. Or stick some on your mirror in your room. Then, when you're fooling with your hair, you'll have a reminder to pray.

You can be as smart as a football player. If one of them can make it a habit to talk to God with 60,000 people watching, you can develop a similar habit in your life.

It's a great way to obey the verse that says, "Pray continually."

On the Chalkboard

No matter what you are doing, God is listening. Pray often.

A Flag on the Pray

In late 2010, a high school player in Texas scored a touchdown on a twenty-three-yard run. After he scored, he knelt down in the endzone and prayed. A referee threw a flag and penalized him for breaking a rule against "players drawing attention to themselves."

Sports Stuff

On the sports teams you have played on, is it popular to be a Christian? Sometimes, even on teams made up of all Christians, teammates will make you feel funny if you try to stand up for Jesus. Yet God has put you on that team for a reason, and it's not to teach you to hide your faith. Being careful not to make a scene, be strong in your faith—even in sports.

How many times do I usually pray in a day? Could I double that? Triple it? Not to show off, but to help my relationship with God.

Devote yourselves to prayer,

being watchful and thankful.

Colossians 4:2

PLAY BOOK ASSIGNMENT:
READ EPHESIANS 3:14–21

The Circle of Prayer

Did you ever hit, grab, slug, tackle, pound, snarl at, and try to defeat someone and then turn around and pray with them? Did you ever kneel down and hold hands in prayer with someone you just spent the last sixty minutes running into, knocking over, and butting heads with?

If you were a football player in the NFL, you could possibly answer "yes" to both of those questions.

Have you ever noticed what happens when an NFL game is over? Of course the coaches race across the field to shake each other's hand, and the TV people grab the star of the game for a quick interview. But there's something else.

Players from both sides meet at midfield, kneel down on the surface, hold hands, and pray.

Sound strange?

Some people think it is. They can't figure out how it can happen. And why.

Although not everyone agrees that it is a good idea, there are at least three things we can learn from Prayer Circle, as it is sometimes called.

First, praying with someone is a great way to overcome differences. Football players may work hard to beat the other team, but those who are Christians can set all that aside when the game is over and focus on what they have in common: love for God.

Second, praying is a way of witnessing about faith in God. Just as your family can witness to others when your dad thanks God for your food in a restaurant, these players are declaring that they believe in God and his power to answer their prayers.

Third, being a strong, tough athlete doesn't mean you don't trust God. Sometimes people think that a tough athlete can't be a strong Christian—that Christians are too meek. But the huge number of Christians who testify of their faith in God through Prayer Circle proves that is wrong.

So, how does this have anything to do with you?

Is there someone you have a disagreement with? Pray with him or her.

Are you bold enough and confident enough in your belief in God to pray in public? At school? At McDonald's?

Do you know that everyone needs to trust God, even the strongest people?

You can learn a lot from watching pro football. Even after the game is over.

effort. Just as a team plays a lot better when the point guard does what the coach says, your life will be more successful if you do as God says.

Get the point?

On the Chalkboard

When you are trying to live for God, the best power to use is "will" power.

A Point Guard to Follow

One of the top point guards in the NBA in the early part of this century has been Chris Paul. He is not only one of the best on the floor, but he's pretty cool off the court too. "It's not really me that is doing all this, but all of the blessings any of us received are through the grace of God," he says. Now, that's pointing the way.

Sports Stuff

If you want to be a successful point guard, you have to have certain characteristics and skills. First, you have to be a very good ball handler. This means spending hours and hours dribbling and passing so you can have complete confidence in yourself. Second, you have to be able to see the entire floor, not just the players near you. You have to notice when your teammates get open and when they need to be redirected. Third, you have to learn to be a coach on the floor. You have to know the plays better than anyone else does, and you have to be able to be bold enough to tell your teammates what they are supposed to be doing.

What decisions did I make recently without even asking God what he thought?

We put up with anything rather than hinder
the gospel of Christ.

1 Corinthians 9:12

PLAY BOOK ASSIGNMENT: READ LUKE 6:42

Bill and Faith

At one time, a guy named Bill Bradley was one of the best basketball players in the country. He led his team, Princeton, to some very exciting victories. Later, he played for the New York Knicks, where he was on an NBA championship team. Even later than that, he got interested in politics and actually ran for president. If you know your US history, you know he didn't win.

Back when he was in college, he was quoted by some publications as saying he was a Christian. He made it clear that he believed the gospel of Jesus Christ.

Something happened to Bradley through the years, though, that changed his mind. Although it's tough to talk about because we hate to see anyone reject the faith, we can learn from the reasons he gave for turning his back on Christianity.

One of the key things he didn't like was what he called *hypocrisy* in the church. Do you know what hypocrisy is?

It's when Christians say they are one thing and act in another way completely.

Like when a preacher speaks out against a certain sin and then gets caught committing that sin.

Or when a church member stands up and says we have to be honest, then gets thrown in jail for taking money from the company he works for.

Or when we say we love everybody, but we talk about our friends like they were our worst enemy. "Hey, did you see Trevor's new shirt? It looks like he got it at a garage sale."

There are lots of people who think the way Bill Bradley thinks. They don't like the way some Christians behave, and they decide they don't want to be associated with us for that reason.

We can learn a couple of things from this former basketball player.

First, we shouldn't be hypocrites. We should be true to our word about who we are. Remember that Jesus didn't like hypocrisy. He said, "Woe to you, teachers of the law and Pharisees, you hypocrites!" (Matthew 23:27). And Peter, writing directly to Christians, said, "Rid yourselves of all malice and all deceit; hypocrisy, envy, and slander ..." (1 Peter 2:1). Someone like Bill Bradley shouldn't look at us and be able to call us hypocrites.

Notice what Paul said: "We put up with anything rather than hinder the gospel" (1 Corinthians 9:12). And being a hypocrite can hinder the gospel.

Second, even if there are hypocrites in the church, that doesn't change the gospel. Jesus' message of hope and forgiveness is what we need to remember. We trust Jesus because of who he is, not because of who the people in the church are.

There will always be people like Bill Bradley—people who are searching for answers but who miss the true answer because of something that draws their attention away from Jesus.

Let's make sure we aren't distracting anyone from Jesus. Let's keep pointing to him. He's the only answer!

On the Chalkboard

People will fail us and disappoint us, but Jesus never fails.

One Big Game for Bradley

Bill Bradley was the Player of the Year in college basketball way back in 1965. In his final game as a collegian, he went out with a bang. Playing against Wichita State University in the consolation game of the Final Four (the NCAA doesn't have this game anymore; it pitted the two losing teams in the semifinals against each other before the final game), Bradley set a Final Four record with fifty-eight points as Princeton beat Wichita State 118–82.

Sports Stuff

Bill Bradley was one of the best pure shooters in college basketball history, and his deadly accuracy was the result of long, long hours of practice. One time when he was warming up for a college game, he thought he noticed that the rims were just a bit too low. Maybe less than a quarter of an inch. So, he mentioned it to his coach. Sure enough, when someone measured the rim before the game, it was discovered to be off by exactly what Bradley said. That kind of eye for the basket comes only through hour after hour of shooting practice. And it points out the importance of making sure the basket you practice on is exactly ten feet from the ground. Don't practice on a short basket just so you can dunk on it.

Instant Replay

When my friends look at me, do they see Jesus or do they see someone who distracts them from Jesus?

It is God who arms me with strength.

Psalm 18:32

PLAY BOOK ASSIGNMENT:
READ ISAIAH 40:30-31

Real Strength

How strong are you?

There are lots of ways to measure that.

You can measure your strength by the number of push-ups you can do.

Or the amount of weight you can bench press.

Or the number of chin-ups you can do.

With some athletes, you can tell how strong they are just by looking at them. You can see their rippling muscles. Or you can watch them do stuff that you know takes a lot of strength and power.

Think of how strong you have to be to be a gymnast. There's the floor routine with its handstands and flips and huge flying-through-the-air acrobatics. There's the balance beam, which requires you to do all sorts of stuff while making sure you don't crash down on your head. There are the uneven parallel bars, with all that swinging and catching yourself and looping around at crazy angles.

Did you ever look at gymnasts' arms? They have pipes!

One of the best gymnasts who ever lived was Mary Lou Retton. In 1984, Mary Lou performed one of the most memorable and awe-inspiring feats in gymnastics history. She was in the running for the all-around championship in women's gymnastics at the Olympics, but she was slightly behind a woman from Eastern Europe going into the final event: the vault.

She would need a perfect vault to win.

With a look of sheer determination, she flung herself toward the vault. She leaped from the springboard, vaulted herself high into the air, turned perfectly, and landed with an absolutely flawless landing. She had stuck a perfect ten.

The event was being held in Los Angeles, and the crowd went crazy. Mary Lou had captured the gold medal.

Today, Mary Lou is a wife, a mother, and a strong Christian. And she recognizes the value of strength. She says, "Physical strength comes from training, lifting one more weight. Or in the case of a gymnast, doing one more flip."

But then Mary Lou makes an observation that is very important to you even if you've never, ever tried to do a reverse flip off the balance beam. She says, "But real courage and real strength comes from God."

Are you any good at memorizing? There's a passage of Scripture in Isaiah 40 that you need to memorize. It talks about the fact that even someone as young as you gets tired, and then it talks about how a tired person can get strength. Real strength. The kind Mary Lou is talking about.

The verses read: "Even youths grow tired and weary, and young men stumble and fall; but those who hope in the LORD will renew their strength."

How strong are you? That all depends on how much you depend on God. He alone can give you real strength—strength of heart and soul.

Feeling weak? Put your hope in the Lord. Then you'll be as strong as Mary Lou! (Although you may not get a gold medal in the Olympics.)

On the Chalkboard

You are only as strong as your relationship with the Lord.

Speaking of Medals

The US women's all-around team was in a similar circumstance in the 1996 Olympic Games in Atlanta. The US team needed a good vault from Kerry Strug to win the first-ever US women's all-around gold medal. Despite an injured ankle, she landed a very good vault, giving the team the gold medal.

Sports Stuff

Does size matter in sports? Of course, you can't play center for the New York Liberty if you are 5' 2", but sometimes it doesn't matter. Mary Lou Retton was only 4' 9" tall and weighed just 92 pounds when she became a world-class athlete. What made the difference for her was dedication. She devoted her time to gymnastics and even moved away from home to dedicate herself totally to it. Although that kind of commitment is not needed for most sports, it does suggest how much a person has to give up in order to become the best. What are you willing to set aside in order to become a better athlete? That's a question you have to ask if you want to be a champion.

Instant Replay

How strong am I spiritually? How can I get stronger?

Consider it pure joy,

my brothers and sisters,

whenever you face trials of many kinds.

James 1:2

PLAY BOOK ASSIGNMENT:
READ JAMES 1:2–8

I Wish Things Were Different

Did you ever have one of those tough days that never seems to end? You know the kind.

Your mom wakes you up five minutes before the bus comes. You leave your homework on the dining room table. Some kindergarten kid drips stuff from his drink box on your science book. Attila the Sub is behind the desk when you walk into the classroom. And you find a note in your locker from your best friend telling you she's now your former best friend.

You know. Worst-case scenario stuff.

Let's be honest. We all have things we don't like about ourselves. Or things we don't like about our lives.

Isn't that right? If you were in charge of things, wouldn't you do some things a little differently?

Here are some of the things that bother us sometimes.

I'm too short.

I'm too skinny.

I'm afraid of crowds.

I'm afraid of spiders.

I can't understand arithmetic (or grammar; it's always one or the other).

I've got bad teeth. Or bad skin.

I can't run fast enough.

Or _____. You fill in the blank.

Let's talk about a girl who had a problem that was her biggest advantage. What was "wrong" with her was something that allowed her to be semi-famous and able to make a lot of money. But first she had to get over having so much of this advantage that she was considered different.

Her name is Katie, and her advantage/problem was that she is very tall.

In fact, there just weren't many girls in the country who were as tall as Katie when she was in high school. She was 6' 8" tall.

That meant that wherever she went, people stared at her. "The attention I got from my height was more than I could bear at times," she recalls. "I was upset when people would laugh or talk behind my back and think I did not hear them."

But being so tall also had its advantages. She got a college scholarship to Liberty University. And then she got a chance to play for a few years in the WNBA.

Do you know of any Bible characters who had a friendship like Shanna and Sidney, two friends who would do anything to help the other?

How about Jonathan and David?

Remember the story of the time Jonathan's father Saul threatened to kill David? Do you recall what Jonathan said to his friend? "Whatever you want me to do, I'll do it for you."

That's what friends do.

Here's a way to remember the idea of being a friend—the way Shanna was for Sidney and Jonathan was for David:

F—Faithful. No question. Your friend will be there for you.

R—Redeemed. Your best friends should be Christians, just like you.

I—Interested. A good friend looks out for you, not for himself or herself.

E—Eager. When you text a true friend, that friend gets right back to you because he or she can't wait to communicate with you.

N—Natural. Friends aren't fake.

D—Discipler. That means you learn from each other as you grow up together.

S—Steady. Not "Oh, I'm mad at you and I don't like you." Instead, "Hey, we can work this out."

On the Chalkboard

It shouldn't hurt to be a friend. Instead, when you are hurt, it helps to have a friend.

Web Testimonies

Both Shanna Crossley and Sidney Spencer put up websites to tell about their ministries. On each of their websites, they give their Christian testimony. Shanna's is *www.szcross.com* and Sidney's is *www.sidneyspencer.com*.

Sports Stuff

One of the reasons Sidney Spencer became such a good basketball player was that she grew up in a family with older brothers who played the game. That meant she always had good competition. It is always good to practice and play games against players stronger and better than you. So, as you try to improve your skills, look for tougher competitors to practice with. It'll make you a better player.

Instant Replay

What can I do for a friend who is in need? How can I encourage him or her?

Even so the body is not made up
of one part but of many.

1 Corinthians 12:14

PLAY BOOK ASSIGNMENT:
READ 1 CORINTHIANS 12:12–26

All Goalies, All the Time

"All right!! Everybody over here!"

It's Coach Pierre of your hockey team.

"Before we go out on the ice, let me go over your positions for today's scrimmage. Van Dyke, you're playing goalie. Robinson, you're my goalkeeper. Keller, why don't you be keeper today? Jefferson, I want you in goal."

You and your teammates look at each other. Has this guy flipped? You can't all play goalie!

277

Who would shoot on the other end of the ice? Who would take the face-offs? Who would slam the other players into the boards?

It's kind of a ridiculous situation, isn't it?

But it's a lot like what the apostle Paul discussed when he talked with the people of the church in Corinth about the job God gives people to do.

The main difference was that he was using the body as the illustration, not hockey (Paul wasn't into hockey, apparently). And what he was trying to point out was that we Christians all have different jobs to do.

Have you ever spent any time at all thinking about what God wants you to do? What part does he want you to have among Christians?

You may think you are too young to know what God wants you to do, but that's not true.

Even if you think only about the different things kids your age can do for God, you begin to learn that not everyone can do the same thing. God has given you a specific skill or gift that you can use for him now.

For example, maybe you are good with a musical instrument. Or perhaps you are a good actor. Maybe you have a lot of Bible knowledge. Or you could be one of those friendly people who has no trouble making new friends. It could be something totally different.

When you begin to notice how different your interests and skills are from others, you are beginning to see what Paul was talking about. God made each of us differently because he has such a wide variety of things that need to be done.

Just like a hockey coach needs some to play center, some to play wing, some to play forward, and some to play goalie, God has us pegged for different jobs in the church.

Begin now to see what God wants you to do for him.

On the Chalkboard

The only person who can fill your spot on God's team is you.

Speaking of Goalies

Sometimes, goalies have it easy. Sometimes they are really, really busy. Sam LoPresti of the Chicago Black Hawks had one of those busy nights on March 4, 1941. While playing against the Boston Bruins, LoPresti was bombarded by eighty-three shots by the Bruins. When the ice chips had cleared, he had given up just three goals. Boston won 3–2.

Sports Stuff

In sports, it sometimes is to your advantage to learn other positions on the team. For instance, a basketball player may need to know how to play the point guard, shooting guard, and small forward positions. If the player can play all three, the coach can put him or her into any of those spots. Study what the other players do; don't learn just your position. It'll make you a better all-around player and give you more of a chance to get into the game.

What do I think God has in mind for me? What are a couple of things I'm good at?

Do not follow the crowd in doing wrong.

Exodus 23:2

PLAY BOOK ASSIGNMENT: READ 2 CHRONICLES 13:4–7

Bad Company

One star basketball player (let's call him Slim) grew up going to church, went to a Christian school through the eighth grade, and had parents who tried to teach him how to live for God.

By the time he graduated from high school, this young star was one of the best players in his state. He was recruited by colleges all over the country.

When Slim finally decided which school to go to, he was joined by several other high school stars. The college team was expected to become national champions because they had so many good players.

At college, Slim was a star. When he teamed up with the other really good players, they became a nationwide powerhouse.

But all was not great for Slim. His new teammates didn't want anything to do with his beliefs or his faith. They started getting him interested in parties and hanging out and doing anything but living for Jesus Christ.

The bigger he got as a star, the less he thought about his faith. After college, he went on to the NBA, where he spent the first several years of his career building a reputation as a troublemaker. He became a player coaches didn't want, and even as someone who got into trouble with the law.

Reflecting on the path that Slim took, his youth pastor from his high school days said simply, "He got in with the wrong crowd, and they led him astray."

What happened to Slim can happen to any Christian. Notice what Paul says in 1 Corinthians 15:33: "Bad company corrupts good character." He was talking specifically about how a person who has wrong beliefs can influence someone with right beliefs to change, but the verse also shows what happens when we hang around with people who aren't godly.

You probably see this happen at school a lot. A new kid comes to your school. You can tell he's trouble, so you stay away. But a friend thinks he's cool, so he starts doing stuff with him. Before you know it, you're saying to your friend, "What are you doing with that guy? You never used to _____ [fill in your own bad habit], but now you do."

It happened to Rehoboam thousands of years ago (2 Chronicles 13:7), and it can happen to you. Don't let it. Don't let bad company make you do bad things.

> *On the Chalkboard*
>
> **A friend who leads you to do wrong is no friend at all.**

Speaking of Influence

Did you know that in most major sports leagues, there is a group of people who are trying to be a good influence on the athletes? These people are chaplains. They hold chapel services and Bible studies for the players of the NBA, NFL, MLB, and the WNBA. This has been a really good influence on a lot of players, for they have someone they can go to and ask for prayer or advice on tough situations.

Sports Stuff

Some athletes have a hard time understanding that their behaviors off the field or court or ice can affect their sports. Here are some ways it can, and what you can do about it.

1. Grades. Many good athletes can't play because they don't have the grades. What to do: Keep up on your daily assignments. Get into the habit of reading. Learn how to study for tests.
2. Discipline. What you do in the classroom or even outside of class will affect how your coach looks at you. What to do: As a Christian, hold yourself to a higher

standard. Perhaps wear a WWJD bracelet to remind you to do what Jesus would do.

3. **Attitude.** If you have a chip on your shoulder, coaches will not want you around. What to do: Stop thinking that everyone is trying to get you. Focus instead on what they are trying to teach you. What do you need to learn?

How can I tell if I'm influencing a person for good or he is influencing me for bad? Who can help me with this?

I can do all this through him

who gives me strength.

Philippians 4:13

**PLAY BOOK ASSIGNMENT:
READ PHILIPPIANS 4:10–13**

I Can Do Everything

Did you ever wonder what the favorite "favorite verse" is among Christian athletes? It's the one on this page.

Of course, there are hundreds of other ones that are cherished by believing men and women in sports, but this one is by far the number one choice.

Why not? Sports are about strength. Sports are about doing. Sports are about getting the most out of your potential.

So, when Christian athletes read a verse that says, "I can do all this through him who gives me strength," it's no mystery why they jump all over it as if it were a hanging curveball.

But what does this verse really mean?

Does it mean that a 5' 3", 102-pound pigtailed shortstop can hit a softball over the 285-foot sign in left field?

Does it mean that a seventh-grade point guard can drive the lane and slam home a reverse dunk?

Does it mean a first-time goalkeeper can stop the other soccer team from scoring every time?

Is this verse a free pass to great athletic achievements?

Nope. This verse really has nothing to do with sports.

What this verse is talking about is doing what pleases God. And it is telling us Jesus is the source for doing what pleases God. If we stay connected to Jesus, we will have the power to do what is right.

Have you ever heard this verse: "When I am weak, then I am strong"? Sounds weird, doesn't it? To be strong, I have to be weak. But that's what Paul said in 2 Corinthians 12:10.

It's true. If we want to have God's strength (to please him, not to hit home runs), we have to admit that we are about as powerful as your grandmother batting against Stephen Strasburg.

Philippians 4:13 isn't like drinking Gatorade. We don't quote this verse as we are stepping to the plate so we can pull a fastball over the left fielder's head for a double.

We quote Philippians 4:13 when we get up in the morning so we can remind ourselves that we can't get to first base spiritually unless we rely totally on Jesus Christ.

We can't avoid temptation. We can't tell our friends about Jesus. We can't grow closer to God. We can't do good things for others. We can't do anything without Jesus! And we can do everything for God with Jesus.

No wonder it's a favorite of so many people.

Trust God's guidelines for living. He knows how to make your life work.

Speaking of Rules

One of the big differences between God's rules and man's rules is that God's rules don't change. Sports rules change. Here are some rules that have been eliminated.

- At one time, you could get a runner out in baseball by throwing the ball and hitting him.
- For a while in the 1970s, it was illegal to dunk a basketball in college and high school basketball.
- Up until about sixty years ago, major league baseball outfielders left their gloves on the field when they went in to bat.
- In basketball's early days, there was a jump ball after every basket.

Sports Stuff

You make the call. To be the best player you can be, you should know the rules of your sport frontward and backward. You can do this by paying close attention to games you play in or watch. Or you can buy a rule book and read it (that's pretty boring to most people). If you are old enough, you might even get a chance to umpire or referee games played by kids a lot younger than you. That will help you learn the rules fast.

Instant Replay

What standards or guidelines bug me? Do I sometimes think I know better than anyone else what I should do? What's wrong with that picture?

For we live by faith, not by sight.

2 Corinthians 5:7

PLAY BOOK ASSIGNMENT:
READ 2 CORINTHIANS 5:1−7

Blind Faith

Like a couple hundred thousand other high school students, Travis Freeman played football. Played center, in fact.

Hike the ball, pick out a defensive lineman, and keep him away from your quarterback. Same routine done by centers on teams all over his home state of Kentucky and all around the country every Friday night.

Except for one thing.

Travis Freeman couldn't see.

Travis lost his sight when he was twelve years old. When he was in middle school, he asked the football coach if he could help out in some supporting position with the team.

The coach said he couldn't do that. But he could play if he wanted. That wise coach saw potential in Travis, and he saw the spark in a young man who wasn't about to let his darkened world snuff out his dream of playing football.

Through middle school and high school, Travis continued to play. By the time he was a senior at Corbin High School, Travis had become recognized across the country for his courage. On Freeman's eighteenth birthday, the National High School Athletic Association presented Travis with the first-ever High School Athletic Hall of Fame Award—and they named it the Travis Freeman Award.

How did he do it? By faith.

Travis told *Sharing the Victory* magazine, "'For we live by faith, not by sight' (2 Corinthians 5:7) is not only a physical verse, but a spiritual one for me. Every step I take is a step on faith, that I'm not going to run into something, that there's actually going to be a floor there. The best definition of faith that I've heard is 'Faith is taking a step in the darkness and trusting that there's going to be ground there. But knowing if there's not going to be ground there, God's going to teach you how to fly.'"

Hey, if he can play football, why not? If Travis can exercise his faith in such a huge way, what does that teach you?

What can you overcome? How hard are you willing to work to be the kind of person people notice because of your faith? And how small do some of your problems seem when compared with what Travis faced when he was twelve?

"God's got a purpose," Travis says. "God has a reason."

What's true for Travis is true for you. Trust God's reasons and work toward his purpose for you—no matter what stands in your way.

On the Chalkboard

Even in life's darkest times, you can trust the Light of the World.

Speaking of Overcoming

The world record for the 100-meter sprint by a non-sighted runner is 11.4 seconds. Graham Henry Salmon recorded that remarkable time on September 2, 1978, in Scotland.

Sports Stuff

You would be surprised to know how many athletes have had to overcome some kind of problem to be really good. Maybe you have something that you think would keep you from succeeding. Before giving up, make sure you do everything possible to compensate for it. Talk with your parents to get their perspectives on it. Give it all you have and you may surprise yourself.

Instant Replay

What challenges my faith?

If I had cherished sin in my heart,
the Lord would not have listened.

Psalm 66:18

PLAY BOOK ASSIGNMENT: READ PSALM 66:16–20

Praying the Right Way

Hall of Fame baseball announcer Ernie Harwell once told this story. By the way, if you have never heard of Mr. Harwell, research him online. He was one of the best announcers ever in baseball history. He worked for the Detroit Tigers until he was in his late eighties. He died in 2010 at the age of ninety-two. Great Christian guy.

Anyway, here is Ernie's story.

The year was 1954 and Baltimore was playing the Chicago White Sox. Catching for the Orioles was Ray Murray. Umpire Ed Hurley stood behind him calling the balls and strikes. With a 3–2 count on the Chicago batter, Hurley called the next pitch a ball, sending the batter to first with a walk.

Murray, who didn't like the call, turned toward Hurley, knelt down, and prayed. He said, "Dear Lord, I know that pitch was a strike. Thirty thousand people in this ballpark know it was a strike. But they have good eyes. Dear Lord, give this poor blind man a pair of good eyes and then he'll know it was a strike."

The umpire threw Murray out of the game.

Is it possible that our prayers can be viewed by God in the same way? Does he ever ignore our prayers?

That's an unusual thought, isn't it? We are always taught that we can pray to God anytime. And we even know that he wants us to pray to him all the time.

So what's this about God not listening—just like that umpire not listening to the praying catcher?

If we have some sin that we are hanging on to and not confessing before God, he doesn't listen to our prayers.

The writer of Psalm 66 seems to be telling us that this is the deal. He talks about what happens when we "cherish" sin. That is, when we treasure a sin and keep it going when we know it is wrong.

Let's say you have been gossiping about a friend—and loving it. You talk behind his or her back, telling all kinds of nasty things about that person. And you can't wait to call your friends and exchange more dirt. That's cherishing sin.

And that will damage your prayer life with God.

So, the first prayer God needs to hear from us when we do that is this one: "God, forgive me for gossiping. Help me to be kind in what I say about my friend."

Then you can read the rest of Psalm 66, which says, "God has surely listened and heard my prayer" (v. 19).

You'll be back to praying the right way.

> **On the Chalkboard**
>
> **Sometimes, the next thing God wants to hear from us is "I'm sorry."**

Speaking of Umpires

Sometimes umpires can be helpful. Stubby Overmire of the Detroit Tigers pitched and won the first game of a doubleheader. After the game, Overmire's wife arrived from out of town, and he wanted to leave to be with her. The Tiger manager told him he couldn't go. Between games, some of the players told the third base umpire about the conflict. In the first inning of the game, the ump walked over to the dugout, looked at Overmire—who was sulking on the bench—and said, "You're out of here!" He kicked Stubby out of the game so he could be with his wife.

Sports Stuff

The best thing to remember about umpires and referees is this short saying by former major league ump Bill Klem: "It ain't nothing until I call it." And remember this: Once an official calls it, there's nothing you can do to change it, so don't look foolish trying.

Instant Replay

Do I have anything going on that is blocking my prayer life from working as it should?

> Whoever claims to love God yet hates a
> brother or sister is a liar.
>
> 1 John 4:20

PLAY BOOK ASSIGNMENT: READ LUKE 15:11–32

Brotherly Love

A long time ago, the Los Angeles Dodgers had two brothers on their team: Norm and Larry Sherry. One day during spring training, the Dodgers were playing an intrasquad game. That's when the team splits up into two groups to play a game against each other.

Norm and Larry were on opposite teams. During the scrimmage, Norm came up to bat when Larry was pitching.

One of Larry's pitches came in high and tight, and Norm went crashing to the ground to get out of the way. As he got up and dusted himself off, he turned to his brother and shouted, "Do that again, and I'll call Mom."

Sound familiar?

Obviously, these two major league players were joking around, but you can imagine that when they were growing up, they had their share of brother-brother squabbles. And many of them probably ended up just like that one.

If you have a brother or sister, you know exactly what this is all about.

"Mom! Michael's in my room!"

"Well, McKenzie hit me and I'm just going after her!"

To which Mom replies, "Michael, don't hit your sister. And McKenzie, stay out of his room. You know the rules."

Of course at that time, she will get the meek reply from both siblings.

"Oh, ok, Mom. We're sorry."

Right. And it's going to rain $100 bills tomorrow!

It's probably more like: "That's not fair! She hit me and I get to belt her one."

Followed by, "MOM! Michael just took one of my CDs."

You get the picture. No, you probably live the picture.

What is the deal with all the fighting between brothers and sisters? Is it because they want their parents to have a heart attack? Are they looking for ways to be grounded? Is it written in their contracts that brothers and sisters have to go at it?

Did you ever think about the Prodigal Son story as a lesson about sibling rivalry? Well, think about it. The younger brother gets his money ahead of time and goes out and blows it. He does what little brothers often do. He makes an immature choice. (Ok, if you're an older sibling, stop gloating.) Then, when young bro comes home, Dad throws a massive party. Guess what big bro does? He gets really jealous.

In both cases, the brothers were each looking out only for themselves. It takes a wise father to help the boys see what's really happening.

Dad tells his firstborn, "Look, I love you too, but you are always here. You have always enjoyed all the great things we have. Your little sib was dead, and now he is alive. Let's party!" In other words, let's get along. You are both well taken care of.

There's a verse in 1 Thessalonians 5 that should be the motto of every brother and sister. It says, "Live in peace with each other" (v. 13). A little brotherly and sisterly love goes a long way at home.

On the Chalkboard

If you have the peace of God in your heart, try letting peace rule your life at home.

Speaking of Siblings

Lots of sibling combinations have played professional sports. For example, did you know that WNBA star Candace Parker (who can dunk) has a brother, Anthony Parker, who spent several years in the NBA? Or that former NBA Reggie Miller has a sister, Cheryl, who played for the US Olympic basketball team (1984) and coached in the WNBA? And they have a brother who played for the California Angels in the late 1980s?

Sports Stuff

Sometimes the best thing a younger sibling has is the example of his older brother or sister. If you have an older brother or sister who is an athlete, watch him or her, learn from him or her. Ask questions about how to get better. And what may help even more, practice against him or her. You'll be surprised how much you'll learn from an older sibling. But you have to live at peace with each other first.

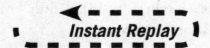

Instant Replay

Do I enjoy irritating my siblings? What can help me realize that this isn't right?

Be diligent in these matters;
give yourself wholly to them, so that
everyone may see your progress.

1 Timothy 4:15

PLAY BOOK ASSIGNMENT:
READ 1 TIMOTHY 4:11–16

Stretching It

Occasionally, I used to go jogging with my kids—all of whom were athletes during high school. Before we ran, there was usually a little ritual that took place before we hit the road. I would walk out to the end of the driveway and wait for everybody else to join me so we could get started. But they were all back pushing against the house or the basketball pole, stretching out their legs.

They would always tell me, "Dad, you have to stretch before you run."

And I would always say, "I've never stretched in my life. I'm not going to start now." And it's true, through high school and college, playing baseball and basketball, I never stretched. I just ran out on the court and started firing away.

But I'm not proud of it. I'm wrong. Fortunate, but wrong.

Most physical trainers will tell you that it's important to warm up, stretch, and then when you're done, warm down. If you don't, funny things can happen to your muscles. Although I never pulled a hamstring or any other muscle (my kids would say it's because I don't have any), I was not training properly.

Stretching is not only good for athletes, but it's also good for Christians. You and I need to stretch our spiritual muscles. We need to find things that will challenge us and make us depend on God more and more.

How can you stretch your spiritual muscles?

It's a matter of devotion (1 Timothy 4:13) and diligence (4:15).

One way to stretch those spiritual muscles would be to decide that you are going to tell an unsaved friend about Jesus. That will stretch you! It's easy to talk to your friend about the other kids at school, about the latest movie, or about some sports star you both like. But it's a major streeeeeeeetch to say, "Do you know Jesus Christ?"

Another way to stretch your spiritual muscle is by making plans to learn something new about the Bible or about faith in general. Let's say, for instance, that you want to know what the Bible says about jealousy. So, you take a notebook, grab a Bible with a concordance, and do a little digging. It's not easy, but it is worthwhile. And it will stretch you!

You can get by without stretching. You can be a Christian who is just doing the basics and getting by. But if you stretch your spiritual muscle, you'll please God, you'll be proud of yourself, and you'll find your faith more exciting.

So, don't do like I do when I go jogging. Take the time to stretch. It'll feel sooooo good.

On the Chalkboard

Expand your spiritual horizons or you'll find your world growing smaller, not bigger.

Speaking of Exercise

One of the greatest generals in US history was Douglas MacArthur. He served in World War II and helped return the Philippine Islands to the control of the United States. Each day, he began his morning with a round of calisthenics. He also walked several miles each day. In his mind, regular exercise was essential for making a person well rounded.

Sports Stuff

According to one of the foremost authorities on exercise and good training, Dr. Kenneth Cooper, here are the basics of stretching:

1. Movements should be done slowly, without bouncing or fast motion.
2. Try to achieve a full range of motion.
3. Work up gradually to your full stretching ability.
4. Hold your maximum stretch for fifteen seconds, then slowly relax.

What can I do that will help me stretch my spiritual muscles?

I gave you milk, not solid food, for you were
not yet ready for it.

1 Corinthians 3:2

PLAY BOOK ASSIGNMENT:
READ 1 CORINTHIANS 3:1 – 2

What's Eating You?

The answer to the question in today's title might be, "What you're eating."

Huh?

"What's Eating You?" is "What You're Eating"? What does that mean?

It means that sometimes what we put into our body doesn't do us much good. Instead, it harms us. Nothing wrong with a nice big Oreo once in a while, but if that's all you were to eat, your body would be a mess. It wouldn't like a full diet of such poor nutrition. In that case, what you were eating would "eat up" your body.

How good are you at knowing what is good for you? Do you think you might do better than a bunch of NBA players? A few years ago, some NBA stars were asked to take a nutrition test. Here are some of the questions:

a. What fluid is best after a game?
b. How much fluid do you need daily?
c. What fluid is best during a game?
d. How much fluid is best one hour before a game?
e. After a late game, which food is best among hamburger, pizza, or Mexican?
f. Before a game, what is the best food to eat?
g. What is the most nutritious kind of pizza?
h. Which dessert is best among chocolate cake, homemade cookies, and banana split?

The athletes got fewer than half the questions right. They didn't know what food and drink was best for their bodies.

Likewise, sometimes we as Christians don't know what is best for helping us grow spiritually. We could ask some questions.

- How much time should I read the Bible each day?
- What kind of music helps me think about God?
- What kind of entertainment choices turn me away from God?
- What are the best kinds of things to read if I want to get stronger in my relationship with God?

Did you read what Paul said in 1 Corinthians? He told the people that they were still eating baby food when they should have been having steak. (Well, ok, he didn't mention Gerber and filet mignon, but that's the point of what he was saying.)

It's easy to develop an appetite for food that is not the best and to be happy with taking a spiritual bottle instead of chomping on meat. But then that makes us spiritual weaklings who can't even make a spiritual layup.

Like those NBA players learned by taking that test, we should learn to eat right spiritually. Then what we're eating will help us grow up the right way.

> ### On the Chalkboard
>
> **Why be on a starvation diet when God has a whole banquet of blessings waiting for us?**

The Answers to the NBA Test

a. orange juice, sports drinks, water

b. 4 quarts

c. water, sports drinks

d. 2 cups

e. pizza

f. chicken and spaghetti; 4 to 6 hours before the game

g. cheese

h. banana split; at least it has potassium

Sports Stuff

Eating well before a sports competition is essential, because that meal (and even the one before) gives you the energy you need. One aspect of this is proper hydration, or taking in fluids. Having proper fluids in your body helps you to not get tired as quickly—that's why you need to drink two cups of liquid an hour before the competition. The meal you want to eat a few hours before competition is one with a solid, high-carbohydrate level.

Instant Replay

Am I hungry spiritually? Am I eating the right things?

We can comfort those in any trouble with
the comfort we ourselves receive from God.

2 Corinthians 1:4

PLAY BOOK ASSIGNMENT:
READ 2 CORINTHIANS 1:3–7

Just a Normal Kid

Sometimes you look at the top athletes in the world, and you wonder how they got where they are. They must have had some kind of special life that allowed them to be so good. Maybe their parents were also world-class athletes and they trained them from Day 1 to be great.

But then you read about a mega track star like Allyson Felix.

Allyson is one of the top runners in the world. She has been in the Olympics (her first one was in 2004), and she has gold and silver medals to prove it. She has won World Championships— with lots of gold medals to show that sometimes she is the very best in the world at the 200-meter race.

But how special was she as a kid?

Let's see. Her mom is a school teacher. Her dad is a seminary professor.

She went to a Christian high school where her friends nicknamed her "Chicken Legs."

She didn't even know she was a good runner until her freshman year of high school.

Pretty much a regular kid who, because God gave her an amazing talent for running fast, became world famous.

And what about now? Now is she some hotshot prima donna person who thinks she's the best thing since sliced bread?

The website Beyond the Ultimate reported this magnificent athlete proclaims, "My faith is definitely the most important aspect of my life."

After becoming a Christian when she was little, she has "continually been striving to grow in my relationship with God. I face struggles every day. My goal is to be more Christlike."

That sounds pretty normal.

And that is great news for you. It should help you keep in mind that if one of the greatest athletes in the world was just a normal kid who grew up to be famous—yet still wants to be a stronger Christian each day—we can do no better than want the same thing.

You don't know yet what great things you might be able to do someday. But you do know that you need to live just like Allyson Felix does now that she's a big star: trusting Jesus with her struggles and trying to grow in her relationship with God.

That should be normal for all followers of Jesus—Olympic champion or not.

> ### On the Chalkboard
>
> **It's not our accomplishments that make a difference; it's how we live for Jesus and trust him that really matters.**

Speaking of Allyson

One of the things Allyson endorses as an athlete is the US Anti-doping Agency's Project Believe program. She is trying to influence the track-and-field world by competing without performance-enhancing drugs and by showing that the best way to compete is to compete clean. She has been called the athlete who can save sprinting because of her clean record and her talent.

Sports Stuff

Even though sprinters don't run very far during competition, that doesn't mean they don't run a lot. One sprinter says that the best thing for him was running ten miles a day. Another thing sprinters have to do is learn how to use the starting blocks. Tips such as starting low and rising slowly, moving hands back and forth and up and down, and keeping the head still are keys to a good start. And a sprinter always leans forward with his or her body—pushing through until at least five yards beyond the finish line.

Instant Replay

Do I sometimes feel unimportant because I'm not a big star? What does it mean to me that Allyson became a strong Christian and was living for Jesus before she became famous and still maintains her faith today?

Greater love has no one than this:
to lay down one's life for one's friends.

John 15:13

PLAY BOOK ASSIGNMENT: READ ACTS 6:8–14; 7:51–60

To Die For

You've heard the phrase "It's to die for." Usually when someone is using these words, that person is referring to an outlandishly delicious dessert or some piece of clothing that was spotted at the mall.

Or it could even be a person.

Rinngg! "Hello." "Hi, Lauren, this is Erica. I saw Corey today at the pool. Whew! He's to die for."

It's a nice little line, and it expresses a feeling of admiration or respect or appreciation for something really nice. But it takes on an entirely different meaning when it is said seriously by someone who has thought about whether something is truly important enough to die for.

Listen, for instance, to one of basketball's all-time best players, David Robinson, as he talks about his love for his Savior, Jesus Christ.

"I'm very convicted, very committed to what I believe. I would die for what I believe. I know about Jesus Christ. I know about the motivation for my life. If I'm not willing to give up my life for the Lord, then there's nothing else in my life worth standing for."

Wow! To Mr. Robinson, faith in Jesus Christ is worth dying for.

That's not something you hear much about these days, is it?

But you probably know about one person in the Bible who gave up his life for Jesus Christ. His name was Stephen, and he stood his ground against the people who were accusing him of doing wrong. In fact, he preached to them about Jesus — more than they wanted to know about Jesus. So much that they grew angry enough at him to kill him.

Although we don't hear much about this kind of thing happening today, it does. There are countries in other parts of the world where Christians are being murdered for their faith right now. Some people have concluded that more Christians were martyred in the twentieth century than in the previous nineteen centuries before.

So, even though the twenty-first century seems like a modern time, people still face something as old and as awful as being a martyr.

You may not ever be called on to defend your faith before a group of people who will kill you if you say the wrong thing, and David Robinson might not ever have to do that either.

But it is important to have that kind of conviction. And most of all, it is vital that we know who is really "to die for"—Jesus.

On the Chalkboard

**Jesus died for us.
The least we can do is live for him.**

More on the Admiral

Since becoming a Christian David Robinson has not been afraid to speak out about his faith in Christ. Here's what he says about that: "The Lord calls different people to do different things. I just happen to have a big mouth, so I like to talk about my faith. I don't like to have secrets. If something is great, I feel I can share it with people. I really have a burden to see people's eyes opened, to see them grow in the Lord."

Sports Stuff

There are lots of different ways to get into shape for your sport. Running, biking, swimming. But David Robinson had a rather unorthodox way of keeping in shape during the off-season when he was still in the NBA. He hiked. He liked to climb hills and explore. So, maybe that will give you another way to get those muscles in tone.

Have I ever thought of what I would do if I were asked to stand up for Jesus if my life were on the line? What would I do?

> What benefit did you reap at that time from
> the things you are now ashamed of? Those
> things result in death!
>
> Romans 6:21

PLAY BOOK ASSIGNMENT:
READ ROMANS 6:19—23

What Happened to Bernie?

You've probably never heard of Bernie Carbo.

That's because you're too young to know about the dramatic home run he hit in the sixth game of the 1975 World Series.

The 1975 Series, some people say, was magical. In fact, on the 100 anniversary of the World Series in 2003, ESPN ranked it the second best World Series ever.

And most would say game six was the highlight of the series.

And Bernie Carbo was a key to that game's greatness.

The Cincinnati Reds had a 3–2 lead over the Boston Red Sox in the Series and a 6–3 lead in game six as the Red Sox came to bat in the bottom of the eighth inning. They put two runners on base for Carbo, who had started his baseball career with Cincinnati and had already hit one home run in the Series. All Bernie did was to step up and pound a game-tying three-run blast into the left center field seats.

Then the Red Sox won the game 7–6 in the twelfth inning when catcher Carlton Fisk hit a home run that hit the foul pole. (You can see a video of both home runs at *www.mlb.com*.)

The Reds won the next game and the World Championship, but that sixth game has never been forgotten by true baseball fans.

For a long time, Bernie Carbo was forgotten. He stuck around the major leagues until 1980, but then he was gone. Washed up at the age of thirty-three. Struggling with a serious addiction to drugs, suffering the death of both parents, and mourning the breakup of his marriage, Carbo was mired in trouble.

In 1992, he decided that life was not worth living. The drugs had drained him of any self-respect or desire. Yet two of his former friends recognized his situation and got him into a treatment program.

It was there that Bernie finally met someone who could help him. A retired preacher told him about Jesus Christ. And a nurse helped him pray to trust Jesus. With a new look at life, Bernie started his own baseball ministry and set off to live for Jesus.

Drugs robbed Bernie of several good years. Jesus gave him hope. What a difference!

Don't ever let anyone tell you that drugs will not hurt you. And don't let a day go by in which you don't thank Jesus for being your Lord and Savior.

What happened to Bernie finally turned out good because he finally met the source of all that is right: Jesus.

"I love Jesus because he gave me new life," says Bernie. Have you received new life from Jesus?

On the Chalkboard

Jesus can protect us from anything our world wants to throw at us.

More about Bernie

After trusting Jesus, Bernie started the Diamond Club Ministry (*www.berniecarbo.com*), which he wanted to use to "tell the greatest story ever told through the greatest game ever played." During his career, Carbo hit ninety-six home runs. He hit twenty-one home runs in his first year with the Reds.

Sports Stuff

Bernie Carbo got started on drugs by taking pills that were made available to him in the clubhouse of major league teams. To keep your body clean and pure, don't experiment with any drugs anyone offers you. Take only the medications prescribed to you by a doctor. Anything that is offered by anyone else as a way of enhancing your performance or in any way relaxing you or making you feel better is dangerous. The pills Carbo started with were performance-enhancing drugs, and he went to worse things from there.

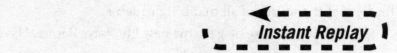

Instant Replay

Am I ever tempted to try substances that I know are not good for me? When I am tempted, how can I let my relationship with Christ protect me?

For if the willingness is there, the gift is acceptable according to what one has, not according to what one does not have.

2 Corinthians 8:12

PLAY BOOK ASSIGNMENT: READ LUKE 21:1-4

Why Give?

How much allowance do you get in a week?

Oops. Did I hear someone say, "None"?

Sorry to open up such a sore spot with you. But hey, you do have some money, isn't that true? You get money for mowing the grass or washing the car or helping Mom with the wash or something! Or perhaps you have a paper route. Or you shovel sidewalks. Somehow, you earn money.

What are you doing with it?

Former major league baseball player Sid Bream was walking along a crowded area of San Diego one day when he met a couple of young boys who were looking for a handout.

When Bream stopped to ask the boys why they were not at home but were out on the street begging, one of them showed him his arms, which had slash marks on them. The boy explained that his dad beat him.

Bream didn't hesitate to pull some money from his pocket and give it to the boys. They had a real need for his help. "I was helping them to show them how much God loved them and how much he loved us," he explained.

But there's more to Bream's giving ways. He also said, "Money, power, and big houses aren't going to mean much when our lives are over and we're standing before Christ."

Have you ever sat down and thought through what God expects of you when it comes to giving? Have you begun to develop a habit of taking some of your money and giving part of it to help God's work?

When you think about the comparison between how much a major leaguer can give and how much you can give, you might begin to think your little bit of money won't do any good.

But that's not the point. The point is that God expects each of us to give out of love for him and concern for his work.

Think about that poor widow Jesus watched as she deposited her two coins in the offering box. She must have known her little gift couldn't feed the poor or help much with the temple treasury. But she gave. And Jesus said, "I tell you the truth, ... this poor widow has put in more than all the others."

Why give? Not to show off or to make a spectacle. But to show our love for God and our concern for others.

You can do that with allowance money, paper route money, or with the money you collect from turning in empty pop cans. It's not the amount, but the heart behind it that counts.

> ### On the Chalkboard
>
> **When you give sincerely and in love, you can't give too much — or too little.**

Speaking of Sid Bream

On October 14, 1992, Sid Bream scored the biggest run of his life. His Atlanta Braves were playing the Pittsburgh Pirates. It was the seventh game of the National League Championship Series. Winner goes to the World Series. Loser goes away, never to be heard from again. Going into the bottom of the ninth inning, Pittsburgh is ahead 2–0. The Braves load the bases. They get one run through a sacrifice fly. Then, with two outs, Francisco Cabrera slaps a hit into the outfield. The runner on third scores with the tying run, but here comes Sid Bream lumbering around third. He has bad knees, so this is not easy. Yet on he chugs. The throw comes toward the plate, Sid slides. He's safe! The Atlanta Braves win the National League pennant.

Sports Stuff

As an athlete and a follower of Jesus Christ, you might sometimes wonder if you can do both successfully. But one thing you have to do is to decide what kind of athlete you are going to be. Sid Bream says Christian athletes should be champions. "I don't think that because we are Christians we should be slack in our competitiveness. I think God wants us to be the very best. I want to show people that Christians are champions."

Have I started making a habit of giving to God's work from all of my money?

- had a career batting average of .286
- won nearly 800 games as a big league manager
- was the National League Manager of the Year

Young Felipe followed his dad, Jose, out into the waters of the Caribbean Sea. Jose absolutely had to catch some fish, for his family had no other food. A storm was coming, and the opportunity for fishing was growing short. Time after time, Jose threw his line into the water, only to come up with nothing. At his side, Felipe begged and begged his papa for one try. Finally, Jose gave his son a chance.

Felipe tossed his line into the water. As soon as it hit, he felt that unmistakable tug on the other end. He hauled in the line, and discovered that a five-pound grouper was attached to the hook. The family would have plenty to eat.

Little Felipe grew up to be Felipe Alou, the player and manager described above. Yet that fishing expedition with his father remained important to him because it has always reminded him to remain humble—that every provision is from God.

In the 1990s, Alou was the manager of the Montreal Expos. This was the team that eventually became the Washington Nationals. In 1994, the Expos had the best record in baseball when the players decided to go on strike. Alou's best chance to make it to the World Series was gone. The team needed money, so they got rid of many of his best players. Later, he also managed the San Francisco Giants, retiring in 2006 at the age of seventy-one.

For a man who was at one time one fish from starvation, this was not a life-and-death problem. He said simply, "The Lord seemed to say to me, 'I didn't send you here to win the pennant; I sent you here to be a witness for me.'"

And that is what he has been. Felipe's fish taught him what is important in life. His baseball team taught him what God wanted him to be. Simple lessons. Simple truths.

On the Chalkboard

It's not the big things in life that show what kind of people we are, but the little things.

More about Felipe

Felipe wasn't the only one of Jose Alou's kids who played in the major leagues. Brothers Matty and Jesus (hey-soos) also played in the majors. At one time, they were all members of the San Francisco Giants. Felipe's son, Moises, became a major league star too. His uncle, Mel Rojas, even played in the majors.

Sports Stuff

Felipe's brother Matty was considered one of the best hitters of his day. He was a slap hitter, meaning he hit the ball all over the field. That worked best for him because he was small (5' 9" and 160 pounds). That is a good technique to learn if you want to hit for a better batting average. To do that, you try to hit the ball where it is pitched. If it is outside, punch it to the opposite field, for instance. This kind of hitter usually knows how to bunt well too.

Instant Replay

What do I consider my major accomplishment so far?

> God is faithful; he will not let you be tempted
> beyond what you can bear.
>
> 1 Corinthians 10:13

PLAY BOOK ASSIGNMENT:
READ 1 CORINTHIANS 10:12–14

Stop the Temptation

Let's talk a minute about something a bit uncomfortable.

Temptation.

Depending on how old you are, you will be tempted by a variety of different things.

All of us are sometimes tempted by things that aren't sinful but might not be so good for us. Like Special Dark chocolate. I could eat a whole bag of Special Dark M&Ms. That wouldn't be a terrible thing to do—in fact, dark chocolate has some healthful stuff in it. But too much sweets is detrimental to a person's body.

And if you are younger, you face different temptations than your older siblings or cousins.

You might be tempted to pick on your sister or maybe even to steal some of your brother's sports cards. And you know both of those things would be wrong.

But the older you get, the more temptations you will face.

Sometimes there are temptations lurking in your house because of the electronics your family owns. As you get closer to being a teenager, you'll realize that the Internet can tempt you to view things you shouldn't see. That's why some families have controls on their Internet. And sometimes texts and photos from friends via cell phones can have images or words that you shouldn't see or read.

The Bible, which needs to be our guide for everything we do, is pretty clear on this somewhat touchy subject. Here's a verse from the book of Job that you need to have in mind as you get older and start to face serious temptation. "I made a covenant with my eyes not to look lustfully at a young woman" (Job 31:1).

Here are some other verses to keep in mind:

"Watch and pray so that you will not fall into temptation" (Matthew 26:41).

"No temptation has overtaken you except what is common to mankind. And God is faithful; he will not let you be tempted beyond what you can bear" (1 Corinthians 10:13).

That's the biblical side. Now the tough part: making it happen.

One pro football player who battled temptation was Jon Kitna, a longtime quarterback in the NFL. Because he knew that he was tempted by the same thing so many guys are tempted by—looking a pictures they should not be seeing—he did something about it.

He has a bunch of people he is accountable to whenever he goes to a hotel. He puts controls on the TV and his computer that keeps him from things he shouldn't visit or watch. And he keeps his wife informed about all of that. He also has his wife's name on all of his credit cards, so he can't rent videos he shouldn't.

Begin now to put controls on the temptations in your life. Honor God by putting no worthless things before your eyes (Psalm 119:37). Run from temptation.

On the Chalkboard

Being tempted isn't a sin; falling to the temptation, though, is.

Kitna's Career

If you are looking for an example of a Christian athlete who can teach perseverance, it's Jon Kitna. He wasn't drafted after his college career, so he had to impress the Seattle Seahawks enough to give him a chance. One way he did that was by going to Europe to play for one season with the Barcelona Dragons of NFL Europe. Finally, the Seahawks signed him, and he became the starting quarterback. Then he went to Cincinnati where he played for a few seasons. He was named the NFL's Comeback Player of the Year in 2003. Next, he went to Detroit, where he threw for 4,000 yards each season, but the Lions were awful. So off he went to Dallas, where in 2010 he was the starter for much of the season after Tony Romo got hurt. At age thirty-eight, he was still playing—despite never being drafted.

Sports Stuff

Do you think you'd be a good quarterback? (Girls can answer these questions too.) Here are some of the characteristics you would have to have:

1. strong hands and good arm strength
2. accuracy in throwing
3. the mental capacity to understand complex plays
4. the ability to look over a defense, figure out what it is doing, and respond
5. toughness
6. leadership qualities
7. a hard head

Instant Replay

What temptations do I struggle with? If I really want help, shouldn't I talk to one of my parents to help me with it?

Share Your Thoughts

With the Author: Your comments will be forwarded to the author when you send them to *zauthor@zondervan.com*.

With Zondervan: Submit your review of this book by writing to *zreview@zondervan.com*.

Free Online Resources at
www.zondervan.com

Zondervan AuthorTracker: Be notified whenever your favorite authors publish new books, go on tour, or post an update about what's happening in their lives at www.zondervan.com/authortracker.

Daily Bible Verses and Devotions: Enrich your life with daily Bible verses or devotions that help you start every morning focused on God. Visit www.zondervan.com/newsletters.

Free Email Publications: Sign up for newsletters on Christian living, academic resources, church ministry, fiction, children's resources, and more. Visit www.zondervan.com/newsletters.

Zondervan Bible Search: Find and compare Bible passages in a variety of translations at www.zondervanbiblesearch.com.

Other Benefits: Register yourself to receive online benefits like coupons and special offers, or to participate in research.

ZONDERVAN.com/
AUTHORTRACKER
follow your favorite authors